Nijole Sadunaite

A Radiance in the Gulag

The Catholic Witness of Nijole Sadunaite

Trans. by Rev. Casimir Pugevicius
and Marian Skabeikis

TRINITY COMMUNICATIONS
MANASSAS, VIRGINIA

ISBN 0-937495-08-5

"Goodness and kindness pursue me every day of my life." (Ps. 23:6)

Table of Contents

Introduction

This is a contemporary, Catholic, counterpart to the *Diary of Anne Frank*. It is the fragmentary story—in her own words —of a very courageous and deeply spiritual woman who at this very moment dares to stand up to tyranny and falsehood, and is willing to pay the price.

The author, Nijole Sadunaite (pronounced knee-YOH-leh suh-DOOH-night-eh), was a year old when Adolf Hitler and Joseph Stalin agreed in the Molotov-Ribbentrop Pact of 1939 to divide Europe between the Communists and the Nazis, bringing on World War II. One of the pawns in the act was Lithuania, a modern democracy about the size of West Virginia, across the Baltic Sea from Sweden, whose population of some 3 million was 85% Roman Catholic. In 1987, Lithuania celebrates 600 years as the last European nation to accept Christianity—the "youngest daughter of the Church".

Nijole was two years old when Lithuania was absorbed by the union of Soviet Socialist Republics. She was three when some 38,000 Lithuanian leaders, intellectuals and peasants were packed into cattle-cars by the Russians on June 14-15, 1941, and deported to a living death in Siberia, the beginning of mass deportations over the next decade, in which one out of every ten Lithuanians were sent to Siberia.

Nijole's earliest memories are associated with the Nazi occupation of her country, 1941-1945, the return of the Russians, and a decade during which Lithuanian partisans courageously resisted the Red Army, waiting in vain for help from the West.

From the first, every effort was made by the Communists to destroy the Church and if possible to uproot the religious faith of the Lithuanian people. Nijole began her formal education in a school system intent on instilling atheism in the children.

The leaders of the Lithuanian hierarchy were killed or imprisoned. Half the churches were destroyed, closed or desecrated; half of the clergy were killed, imprisoned or exiled; all religious orders, church institutions, publications and organizations were suppressed. Those who continued to practice religion became second-class citizens.

The terror continued after Stalin's death. Bishop Vincentas Sladkevicius was exiled from his diocese in 1959, and Bishop Julijonas Steponavicius in 1961. The newly built Church of Mary Queen of Peace in Klaipeda was confiscated and converted into a concert hall in 1961, and the clergy who built it were imprisoned. By the time Nijole was a young woman, national and Church resistance to the Soviets in Lithuania appeared broken.

Then, during the 60's, a spiritual renewal gradually manifested itself, leading to the appearance of the clandestine *Chronicle of the Catholic Church in Lithuania*, and a score of other Lithuanian *samizdat* ("self-published" material, without government approval).

Since then, there have been scores of petitions, signed by hundreds of thousands of Lithuanians, who brave harassment by the KGB and worse to demand their rights under Soviet and international law. There have been other signs, too, of stiff religious resistance to the imposition of atheism on a population with deeply Catholic roots, including the Lithuanian version of the Solidarity movement (although there seems to be no formal connection with that Polish phenomenon).

Nijole Sadunaite has been a leader in the contemporary revitalization of Catholicism in Soviet-Occupied Lithuania. This is her story, in her own words, which she entitled *How I Became a Target of the KGB*.

Dr. Thomas Bird
Professor of Slavic Studies and Political Science
Queens College of the
City University of New York

Publisher's Note: This book has been edited into a unified whole from separate manuscripts smuggled out of Lithuania over a period of years and translated under the auspices of Lithuanian Catholic Religious Aid in New York. To provide detailed information about the nature of the manuscripts and the manner of their arrival would only jeopardize those who have risked much to make their publication possible.

PART I: PREPARATION

A Catholic Family

My father, Jonas Sadunas, born September 8, 1899, was the youngest in a large family. Five of them reached maturity: four brothers—Juozas, Sylvestras, Kazimeras and Jonas, and a sister, Ursule. They were born and reared in the village of Pusne, District of Giedraiciai, County of Ukmerge. He was intelligent, decent and very industrious. Working as a herder for a long time, he prepared himself for and successfully completed the gymnasium final examinations.

In 1924, he enrolled in the Department of Agronomy at the Agricultural Academy, passed all his semester and final examinations, completed a year of practicum, defended his thesis and, in 1930, the Jubilee Year of Vytautas the Great, on September 5, he received his diploma as a qualified agronomist and remained as a teacher in the same agricultural academy of Dotnuva. He was religious, but he became especially strong in his faith, so that when he visited Lourdes, in France, he could have joyfully died for God. That was Our Blessed Mother's gift to Dad.

During vacation, my father used to travel extensively with Professor Ruokis Ruseckas: they travelled all over Western Europe and visited Africa. He had a great love for the poor, and he used to help them greatly, because he had experienced much hardship himself while studying.

On May 10, 1934, he married. My mother, Veronika Rimkute-Saduniene, was born in early September, 1915, into a large family. There were eight children, among them an orphan cousin who later graduated from medical school. One brother, Aloyzas, died as a young child. Everyone used to say that such children do not live long. The good God took this little angel to Himself.

Mother was born and reared in the village of Juozapava, District of Svedasai, County of Ruokiskis. Like Dad, she was intelligent, industrious and deeply religious. She graduated from the gymnasium of Borsiai, and after marrying, enrolled in the Agricultural Academy of Dotnuva.

In the evenings, she liked to walk with my father along the park pathways. Students would hide behind the bushes trying to hear what the newlyweds were talking about, and they were greatly surprised to hear that the two of them recited the rosary as they walked along. On Friday, March 22, 1935, a son was born, whom, on May 12 in the Roman Catholic Church of Dotnuva, they christened Jonas Aloyzas.

Later, while expecting me, Mother contracted pleurisy. To save Mother's life, the physicians advised her to have an abortion. She would not agree, saying, "God alone is in charge of all life, and His will be done."

Early on the morning of Friday, July 22, 1938, I came into the world screaming loudly. I was born in the hospital which used to be on Donelaitis Street, in Kaunas. Mother bore me, like my brother, without pain, and so she used to tell me that as soon as she saw me, she looked at me lovingly and called me fortunate. Now the physicians unanimously agreed that only the birth had saved my mother's life!

After my birth, Mother was transferred to the sanitarium to recuperate, and Dad brought me home. He raised me with the help of his sister, Ursule, who spoiled me greatly. On October 2, in the Catholic Church of Dotnuva, Canon Kemesis baptized me Felicita Nijole. He was later arrested, and after being tortured, died in a Soviet prison. May he rest in the joy of the Lord!

I was already nine months old and walking, when mother returned from the sanitarium. Sometime later, she suffered from exposure to the cold on the way to church and contracted tuberculosis of the bone. This belated diagnosis was made when she slipped a disk; at that time she was admitted to the hospital where she lay motionless about three months. The disk slipped back into place, but did not have time to calcify properly.

The war broke out and we had to bring her home from the hospital. In 1941, Dad was informed that he and the family were slated by the Soviet occupiers for Siberia. Placing my mother, who could not walk yet, in a wagon with me and my brother, Dad got as far away from home as possible. In this way, the good God saved our family from death. In those days, men being exiled to Siberia used to be separated from their wives and children, and almost all of them died of starvation in the Siberian taiga. So the Soviet occupation authorities sentenced me to death in Siberia the first time when I was not quite three years old. And what for? Just because I had decent parents who loved God and people! After all, every decent person is the greatest enemy of the Soviets because he will never be enslaved to falsehood!

It was difficult for Dad with a sick wife and two small children, without shelter and without a source of income. A helping hand was extended by His Excellency, the Martyr-Bishop Vincentas Borisevicius of sacred memory, who engaged him to teach at the seminary in Telsiai, and arranged a place to live and food for the whole family. I was of a very lively temperament, according to my mother; like quicksilver unable to sit still. Mother, concerned for my future, took me to the Cathedral of Telsiai and commended me to the Blessed Mother, whose special protection I feel to this day, and to whom I am grateful from the depths of my heart for everything.

On June 10, 1945, Jesus came to my undeserving heart for the first time in the Blessed Sacrament. That same day, Bishop Vincentas Borisevicius conferred on me the Sacrament of Confirmation, while the bishop's sister, Maryte, became my confirmation sponsor.

Among my childhood impressions from those days, the image of Bishop Borisevicius stands out, bright as that of a saint. He stood out among all others in goodness and simplicity. His sister told me that Bishop Borisevicius prayed to God from his youth for the gift of martyrdom, as the greatest grace. His prayer was heard. In 1946, he was arrested and for long months, tortured in the cellars of the KGB. When his sister Maryte would take food and clothing to be handed on to him, they used to give her Bishop Borisevicius' torn and blood-soaked clothing. On a few occasions, the clothing was soaked in sewage and, in laundering, gave off a very foul odor.

More than once, they kept Bishop Vincentas in a punishment cell full of sewage, and when he lost consciousness, they would pull him out. All those articles of clothing I saw with my own eyes. New linen bore great bloodstains, and was torn to ribbons. So terribly did they torture Bishop Vincentas in their desire to force him to consent to falsehood. They were unable to do so; he remained faithful to God and the truth.

For this, on August 26, 1946, he was libeled by the KGB in the Supreme Court of Vilnius and condemned to death. His sister, Maryte, touched him as they took him past her. There was no flesh, just skin and bones; but from his tortured and emaciated face radiated peace and joy and he smiled at his sister. During his trial, he uttered just one sentence, "Before God and man, I am innocent!"

A student who had been in the death cell with the bishop and had miraculously survived, told me that Bishop Vincentas strengthened them all spiritually, explaining the truths of reli-

gion, giving conferences, and spending most of the time in recollected prayer on his knees. Whenever he received a small
packet of food, he immediately divided it among everybody,
leaving nothing for himself. When they would take him out for
interrogation, apparently they were always expecting to break
his faithfulness to the truth. He would leave as if on his way to
death, blessing everyone.

More than once, they threw him back in the cell uncon-
scious. They would place steel plates on either side of his head
and press them together until he lost consciousness. But they
were unable to enslave the powerful spirit of the bishop to
falsehood. Then once, his blessing was final: They took him
from the cell and never brought him back.

His Excellency, Bishop Vincentas Borisevicius, and Father
Pranciskus Gustaitis were shot at the foot of Gediminas Hill in
Vilnius, in the yard of the barracks standing beyond the Vilnele
River. Early in the morning they brought them in a covered
truck, lifted them both out because they could not stand,
jammed them back-to-back like shocks of wheat, and killed
them with pistol shots to the temple. When they slumped to the
ground, they were kicked over on their faces. Their hands, tied
with rope behind their backs, were freed when the ropes were
cut with a knife. With a few more kicks, the bodies of the martyrs were pushed into a grave which had been dug right there.
The soldiers immediately filled the grave, and covered it over
with yard dirt, so that no sign would remain of the burial.

The date and place of the execution was leaked by a KGB
agent, who had purposely worked there so that he might help
the prisoners as much as possible, to a relative of his, who like
all Lithuanians of good will, held the bishop in high esteem.
Early that morning, she went up to Gediminas Hill and hid in
the shrubbery. She saw everything herself, and later told me. "It
was so terrible that for a long time, I could not sleep, I was so
shocked. I can still see it all. . . . I would never go again to see
it. . . ."

In the words of our Martyr-Bishop Mecislovas Reinys: "Happy are those who have not bowed to falsehood, they live forever! They reinforce our ranks!" All you holy martyrs of Lithuania, pray for us!

We lived in Telsiai until the end of 1945, and when the KGB began looking for Dad, we immediately left Telsiai in secret for Anyksciai. There, a good friend of Dad's, Antanas Slamas, was employed as Director of the Experimental Station at Elmoninkai. He took Dad on as a senior research assistant. We went to live with mother's aunt in Anyksciai, and later obtained an apartment in the suburbs—in Jonydsenos.

Around us was a stand of pine, and nearby, the River Sventoji. Dad used to go to work on a bicycle, and in winter, on horseback. His place of employment was five kilometers away. We experienced much hardship, and even starvation. Dad used to earn in a month just enough to buy three kilograms of butter. There was a shortage of bread. Sometime later, some good people gave Dad a cow to support himself. In the garden, he used to grow potatoes and vegetables. We got back on our feet, but whenever we heard automobile motors roaring early in the morning, we would all run out into the grain fields to hide, lest they take us off to Siberia. This is how most Lithuanians lived, as if on the rim of a volcano.

At our nextdoor neighbor's was the headquarters of the Communist irregulars. Words fail me in describing their cruelty. Here they used to torture partisans, and throw their terribly mutilated corpses out in the yard, next to the well from which we used to draw water. Later, those corpses used to lie for weeks in the town square of Anyksciai. They were not allowed to be buried. They used to kill people without compunction. Often, if peasants just visited their neighbors, the irregulars used to consider them partisans, and shoot them. The word "irregular" (*stribas*) became a curse-word, so repelled were people by their deeds.

All Lithuanians of good-will loved the partisans, sympathized with them and helped them as much as they could. Partisans used to come also to the Elmoninkai Experimental Station. Always polite, pleasant and cheerful, upon departure they would leave the director a receipt for the government grain, etc. which they had taken, so that he might have something to present to the irregulars. The infuriated irregulars used to guard the Elmoninkai Experimental Station for weeks, and when they lost patience and pulled out, the partisans would come back and again leave a list of what they had taken from the government granary.

At that time, there was not one Soviet turn-coat at the experimental station, not a single Party member. Soviet officials used to call the Elmoninkai Experimental Station the "bandits' station". Director Antanas Slamas had to exhibit much tact in order to placate the Soviet officials and others who would come in looking for trouble. Most often, it was possible to calm them down by entertaining them and getting them drunk. Director Slamas saved many people. May God reward him with eternal happiness!

The Beginnings of Resistance

At school, the teachers pressured me and my brother to enroll in the Pioneers and, later, the Communist Youth League. They used to keep me until midnight in the faculty room, and the Party activist Ubagevicius tried to force my brother and other pupils, with a pistol, to write petitions to the Communist Youth League. Because we did not acquiesce to force, they expelled us from school.

Summoned to school, my mother told them, "If the only ones allowed to go to school are Pioneers and Communist Youth League members, my children won't go to school. It would be better for them not to finish school, but to grow up to be decent people. They're not going to be hypocrites and compromisers!"

After two weeks, the teachers themselves invited us to return to school. Our mother's firmness had successfully defended us. Oh, how many mothers in those days did not dare to defend their children!

When I was in school, I especially liked sports. I was on school basketball, volleyball, and table tennis teams and participated in track meets. This conditioned me physically. And since we grew up on the banks of the Sventoji, we used to swim until late fall.

Every Sunday and Holy Day, the whole family used to participate in the Holy Sacrifice of the Mass, and listen to the sermon. To this day, I remember the sermons of our pastor, Father Vincentas Arlauskas, of sainted memory. He accurately compared the militant atheists with the hog under the oak tree, in the story by Krilov. The hog filled up on acorns which had fallen from the oak tree into the mud, and began rooting around the oak. He did not know enough to lift his snout up from the dirt to see from where the acorns fell. So it is with the atheists. They make use of all the gifts God has given them: intellect, health, the blessings of nature, but they want to get rid of the very Giver of all those gifts. However, just as the hog was unable to root up the oak, but only to bloody his snout against its roots, so it is with the poor atheists. . . .

May the Lord grant eternal bliss to Father Vincentas for his noble work in struggling against the plague of atheism. His sermons which I used to listen to so attentively, his conversations with my parents, helped me not to get lost in the darkness of atheistic education. I used to enjoy greatly reciting the Office of the Blessed Virgin Mary during the early morning Mass. I never missed Mass on Sundays, even when games were scheduled in other cities. For that conscientiousness, I am grateful to my saintly parents.

Every evening, we used to kneel down for prayers in common, which were led most often by Dad. During May, I used to put up something like a little altar in my room: We used to decorate the picture of the Blessed Mother with flowers, and even the neighbors used to come and pray with us.

Canon Petras Rauda—may the Lord grant him eternal happiness—consecrated our family solemnly to the Sacred Heart of Jesus. He also blessed my parents' marriage-of-Saint-Joseph. Mother, suffering from tuberculosis of the bone, was unable to have children, so she and Dad agreed to live as brother and sister. They lived this way the rest of their lives.

Dad respected my mother very much, and loved his family. His patience, industriousness, self-sacrifice and cheerfulness were for us the best unspoken sermon.

From the war years, when the Blessed Mother saved his life, he daily used to recite the fifteen decades of the rosary. This is how it happened:

During the war, we found ourselves near the front. Soviet soldiers took Dad's bicycle, which had been left by the house. He caught up with them and tried to convince them how much he needed the bicycle, asking them to return it. The soldiers angrily declared that he was a "bandit", and they wanted to shoot him on the spot, behind some bushes. Dad mentally commended himself to the Blessed Mother, asking her help, and promising in thanksgiving to recite the fifteen decades of the rosary daily in her honor. He feared not so much for himself, but for us.

At that instant, an officer appeared from somewhere, and asked the soldiers about my Dad. Then he demanded to see my father's papers and, convinced that he was not guilty of anything, released him. Dad kept his promise until his death; in thanksgiving to the Blessed Mother, he used to say the entire rosary daily.

He was very spiritual, like a priest. Even the Communists in Anyksciai use to say, "We know that Jonas Sadunas is a priest. But how come he has a wife and children?"

My mother also was very saintly. She loved God with all her heart, and offered the pain of her illness for me, so that being of a very lively temperament, I would not go astray. I thank God with all my heart for the saintly parents given me! My father, by his prayer and sacrifice, obtained the grace of God for his children. I understand very well that not a single person would have gone astray in the night of Soviet falsehood if he had parents like mine. So, to whom much is given, of him much will be required. May the good God be merciful to me!

In 1953, my brother finished middle school, and that same year, enrolled in the Agronomy Department of the Lithuanian

Agricultural Academy. In 1958, he graduated from the academy, receiving a degree as a scientific agronomist.

In 1955, I completed Jonas Biliunas Middle School, in Anyksciai. The question arose where to find the shining light of happiness, not just for myself, but also for others. When I received my diploma from middle school, Dad said to me, "Nijole, remember that every person needs health, a good name, and bread to live, but more necessary than anything is faith in God. I would gladly renounce everything else and die in prison or in Siberia, but I would not deny my faith in God before even one individual, because this is God's greatest gift to a person."

Those words still ring in my ears, all the more because they have been borne out by the whole noble example of my parents' lives. Mother and Dad used to assist at the Holy Sacrifice of the Mass and receive Holy Communion every Sunday and Holy Day throughout Stalin's reign of terror. Oh, how well they could pray—they practically immersed themselves in God. Many times, Soviet officials threatened to dismiss Dad from his position, on account of his open attendance at church. "Then I'll go to work as an ordinary laborer," Dad used to say calmly. He trusted God, and God protected our family.

All people of good will loved and respected Dad; his co-workers and even some Communists were impressed with his firmness of character. He was elected for two consecutive terms as Peoples' Deputy of the Anyksciai *Rayon*. The Communists used to say that the villagers would not heed them, and did not trust them, but when Dad spoke, they believed him. Dad was concerned with easing the peasants' lot. He obtained permission for people to hold larger pieces of land, and keep more animals. He knew how to bear up under all attacks with good humor, in that way disarming even his enemies.

When I finished middle school, I had the opportunity to enroll in the Institute of Physical Culture to become a teacher or a trainer. But that meant renouncing religious practice and being a hypocrite in the eyes of people, since only atheists can be Soviet teachers. No, this was not my style! God is the source of every individual's happiness, and without Him, there is no real happiness in life.

The thirty-two years of my life since then have demonstrated that truth. For the fact that I understood it in my early youth, I am very grateful also to His Excellency, the Exile-Bishop Julijonas Steponavicius, saintly priests and Brone Kibickaite.

Brone and I lived in the same house, and went to the same school. On July 26, 1956, during the Feast of Saint Ann, His Excellency Bishop Julijonas Steponavicius administered the Sacrament of Confirmation. Brone asked me to be her sponsor. I agreed. Before conferring the sacrament, Bishop Steponavicius vividly explained that those being confirmed should be consciously prepared to receive the Holy Spirit. I felt that I lacked its grace very much and asked Brone to turn over half of her gifts from the Holy Spirit. She agreed.

Right after the Sacrament of Confirmation, we both felt interior upheaval, a clear understanding of the purpose of life and great happiness. Late into the night, we walked together through the Grove of Anyksciai, amazed at the wondrous working of the Holy Spirit. That was the happiest day of my life! We both found the light of happiness: To God alone belong our hearts in their entirety! Only God is the goal of every human being, and the great source of happiness.

Even Mother, unable to understand such a sudden change in me, thought that I had thought up a new game. Mother loved the way of life I was choosing, only she feared lest it be a thoughtless game on my part. She supported me with her prayers and blessing. How grateful I am for everything to Mother and Dad! On my account, they later had to experience much unpleasantness. In the Soviet newspaper *Komjaunimo Tiesa (Truth, Communist Youth League Edition)*, an editorial writer bemoaned the fact that apparently my father took me, a bright, energetic, happy athlete, and shut me up in a convent.

First Secretary Lukosevicius of the Anyksciai *Rayon* Lithuanian Communist Party Committee berated my Dad more than once, and sent for me. When my father and I went to see him, he began to carry on and scold Dad.

I could stand it no longer, and admonished him, saying that as Dad's junior, he had no right to shout and scold so. "It is a shame to speak such nonsense, as though in the twentieth century, parents could shut up an energetic eighteen-year-old girl somewhere. After all, you know well that I'll get out through the smallest opening if you try to confine me.... Please stop terrorizing my father!"

For some time after my return, I lived with my parents and the militant atheists calmed down. The poor things did not know that it is not within their power to take away the grace of God, and that there is no such power in the world. I helped Dad with his work. He had just had a hernia operation and could lift nothing heavy. Mother, an invalid with a deformed disk, suffered greatly but was always very patient and cheerful. On Dad's sixtieth birthday, his co-workers and the director congratulated him. Here is a citation from Order No. 141 from the director of the Elmoninkai Experimental Station, dated September 11, 1959:

"To Senior Research Associate, Comrade Jonas Sadunas, son of Juozas, on the occasion of his sixtieth birthday, for his long years of conscientious work at the Experimental Station of Elmoninkai, and for his successful work, I express my thanks and wish him health and long years of fruitful labor." It was signed by Director Antanas Puodziukas.

Less than a month later, another order arrived from the Soviet "inside", not without pressure from the KGB. It was Order No. 170 of the Agricultural Scientific Research Institute of Lithuania, October 8, 1959: "It has been decided to terminate Jonas Sadunas, son of Juozas, Senior Research Associate at the Elmoninkai Experimental Station, on October 15, 1959, as having attained retirement." It was signed by Petras Vasinauskas,

Director of the Lithuanian Agricultural Scientific Research Institute of Pasvalis.

To Dad, this was an unpleasant blow. He liked his work, and the people with whom he had worked for so many years; but he did not feel sorry for himself, or complain. He knew how to bear up under all life's blows, silently and patiently. It only made his noble soul shine more brightly.

When they forced Dad into retirement, I was living and working in Vilnius. I could find no room for my parents to rent. I found an apartment in Riese, seven kilometers outside of Vilnius. In order that they might register me there, I obtained work in the hospital of Kalina. Then Mother and Dad came to live with me. Once again we were living together. Dad happily served at the altar during the Holy Sacrifice of the Mass every Sunday and on weekdays. For this, he once more attracted the ire of the authorities.

The bureaucrats berated him and threatened to take away his pension, saying that it was embarrassing for a former scientific associate to serve in church. To this, Dad replied that they could keep their pension, and that there was no greater honor for a man than to be able to serve with the priest at the altar. "I'm not worthy of it. . . ."

Seeing that he did not become frightened, they left him with his pension and never threatened him again.

All his life, Dad begged God for the grace to be allowed to die a painful death, like the Good Thief on the Cross, just so that immediately after death, he could be with the Lord. God heard his prayer. On April 28, 1963, on his way to church, he was run over by a truck. His skull was fractured, his knee was shattered and his liver was crushed. For a whole day, he suffered very patiently, praying and making Acts of Contrition in the Vilnius I Hospital. At 11:00 AM on April 29, he fell asleep in the Lord.

His face radiated peace and joy. His friends said that even while alive, he had never been as beautiful as he looked laid out in the casket. He died at the age of sixty-three. Blessed are those who die in the Lord. May they rest in the joy of the Lord forever. On May 1, 1963, we interred him in the Cemetery of Riese.

A Circle of Suffering

That same year, Dad had been arranging to bring Grand-mother, my mother's mother, home from Siberia. The Soviet occupation forces had exiled my mother's parents to Altay, Siberia. Their great-grandparents had been serfs and like most Lithuanians, very industrious. During the years of Lithuanian independence, my mother's father obtained a loan from the bank, and with some other farmers, bought on auction a piece of farmland from the estate of a Polish nobleman who had gone bankrupt. Grandfather and his children built themselves a home, working like ants from morning until night. They were very religious and upright. People who used to work for my grandparents during the busy season told me that they were like real parents to everyone. Everyone ate the same food at a common table, worked together, and the wages were very generous. "We used to get more in a day than they do in the communal farm in a month," one woman told me with tears in her eyes. "They were better to me than my father. . . ." That woman is still living in Svedasai.

They respected and loved my grandparents not only in Lithuania, but also in Siberia. The Siberians considered Grandfather Juozapas to be a clergyman: We used to pray together, he would explain various questions, and people used to come to

25

him for advice. My grandfather died and was buried in Altay. On his grave, they erected a cross of birchwood. May he rest in the joy of the Lord, for he forgave from his heart everyone who had wronged him.

Relatives brought Grandmother Karolina back to Lithuania in 1963. For some time, she lived with us. At that time, we were living at Varsuvos 13-1 in Vilnius (next to the Cemetery of Rasiai). We were renting an apartment consisting of a half-basement, an unheated and damp room, and a kitchen in which we lived. Mother loved and respected Grandmother very much. In 1964, along with all of Mother's illnesses, she contracted rheumatoid arthritis after being exposed to cold. She was very ill. She often perspired greatly. The joints of her hands and feet became deformed. She spent five and a half years in bed.

The apartment was very poor, and in spite of the fact that Mother was a Group I Invalid, and had priority, we waited for a cooperative apartment more than five years. On one occasion, some visitors from abroad came to visit Mother and were so shocked that we were living in such a hole that for a long time, they did not dare enter the kitchen. "Back home, even the blacks have better apartments," they said.[1]

Once we received a visit from my cousin who, seeing our miserable living conditions, offered to take Grandmother to live with her. Her family (of five) and her mother and father, had an entire frame house of government issue. We had been informed that we would not get a cooperative apartment that year, so we parted with Grandmother, thinking that she would be better off with her other daughter and granddaughter. There she would have a private, warm room. After some time, Grandmother fell ill. My cousin and aunt nursed her lovingly but her exhausted body could no longer resist the illness and Grandmother fell asleep in the Lord. May she have eternal rest.

---

[1]Second-class citizenship of blacks in the U.S. is a recurring theme of Soviet propaganda.

Mother could not attend the funeral, since she herself was seriously ill, confined to bed.

After much effort running between offices, on December 23, 1969, we obtained a cooperative apartment at Architektu 27-2 in Lazdynai. Almost all the loan for the cooperative apartment had been provided by my brother who, since 1968, had been working as a senior agronomist in various places. He lived alone, frugally, loved Mother very much and did what he could to get an apartment.

While working at the Experimental Station of Voke as Senior Agronomist, he caught cold and the doctor forbade him to work in the fields. So in 1971, he obtained employment at the Lithuanian Ministry of Agriculture in Vilnius as Senior Agronomist-Economist. They assigned him a room in the apartment with us and Mother. This is how we got a three-room apartment.

All this time, I was an ordinary factory worker and took care of Mother. Mother was not able to enjoy the new apartment for long. Six months later, on June 16, 1970, she fell asleep in the Lord, only fifty-four years of age. She prayed for and received from the Lord an easy death. All her life, from the age of twenty-three, she had been seriously ill, but she went to the Lord without pain. According to Doctor L. Sinvak of happy memory, who treated her, she died of tubercular meningitis. Mother knew how to suffer and to love. For everything and at all times, she was thankful to God.

Brone Kibickaite, who prayed with me and my brother at Mother's bed as she was on the way to her eternity, and helped prepare her for the wake, wanted very much to at least glimpse where Mother was now. That night when we all went to bed, Brone heard beautiful music, and singing such as she had never heard. She sat up in bed, and the music and singing ceased. As soon as she lay down, the music resumed. This happened three times. Brone told me, "Your mother is in heaven. I was not able to see her but I did hear how beautifully they sing there. . . ."

We interred her in Riese.

After working in the computer center of the University of Vilnius, I finished nursing school and worked in the Children's Home in Vilnius, where they kept foundlings and orphans up to the age of three. Poor little children, how much they need the love of a good mother! Moreover, I got to take care of Canon Petras Rauda, Mother's former chaplain, who was very ill at the time. Because he would not submit to falsehood, he suffered for thirteen years in the Soviet Gulag. He returned swollen from starvation, virtually toothless and almost blind. He did not even wish to recall the hell he went through, but his spirit was unbroken, and he not only remained faithful to the truth himself, but he taught others to trust in God alone and to work boldly for the good of God and country.

He forgave everyone, loved everyone and prayed for everyone. Very patient, he was aware that he was suffering from cancer of the stomach, and that he would never recover, but was always calm and cheerful. He prayed humbly: "Even if I die in the most distant corner of the world, Lord, just let me be with You for all eternity!"

And when his former pupils, now physicians, shed tears at seeing him so emaciated, he smiled and said, "You must rejoice, and not weep. When you let your children go for vacation with their grandparents in the village, you are glad that they get a rest. I'm getting ready to go to the good Father of us all. So you must not weep, but rejoice!"

He had the ability of cheering others and comforting them, right up until death. Even though he suffered much, he refused any sedatives, bearing all the pain. He prayed especially for the priests in Lithuania, whom he loved very much, and every day he prayed for Russia. He was grateful to everyone for the slightest service. I used to wonder how someone suffering so much could take notice of others and, right up until death, be concerned for their welfare. Only people of great spirit are able to live and die in this way.

Canon Petras Rauda fell asleep in the Lord on March 7, 1974. May he rest forever in the joy of the Lord.

My brother's wife Maryte also suffered much. They exiled her as a thirteen-year-old in 1948, together with her parents and her sister, three years older. What for? Their family lived in the District of Marijampole, three kilometers from the town of Kalvarija, on the banks of Lake Oreja. One day, it was raining very hard and three partisans passing by stopped in their barn to get out of the rain. Someone saw and reported it. Immediately, irregulars showed up, killed the partisans and took their whole family away. They beat the father severely, tortured him, kept him in prison and later sent him separately to concentration camp. Exhausted by his sufferings, he died. May he rest in God!

Maryte, only thirteen years old, in the Siberian taiga not far from Irkutsk, had to carry two pails of sap each trip to the collection point. Everyone suffered from hunger and from cold. The mother's legs became paralyzed. Later, Maryte, through great trials, completed nursing school in Irkutsk, and returning to Lithuania in 1958, completed a correspondence course at the Medical Institute of Kaunas. She now works in the polyclinic as an eye doctor. Since Maryte herself saw great hardship from childhood, she is now capable of sympathizing with all who suffer, and helps them as much as she can. The sick love and appreciate her greatly. May God help her do even more good for people.

PART II: ORDEAL

The Crime

During my twenties I worked at the most menial tasks, holding clerical and factory jobs, so I could go to church and pray without trepidation. In 1970, however, I took work in the computer center of the University of Vilnius Physics and Mathematics Department under the title of Senior Engineer, with the duties of key-punch operator, earning about 100 rubles a month. But I had to leave that position because the university rector called me in and told me that if I did not resign, it would go badly for him. I did not want him to suffer, so I drafted my resignation, and they terminated me "at my request". Here is what happened. . . .

In 1970, when a criminal case was brought against Father Antanas Seskevicius for catechizing children, I hired an attorney for him. But to sympathize with and help those who are being persecuted by the KGB is to make oneself a target of the KGB.

Father Seskevicius' trial took place in Moletai on September 7 and 8, 1970. When we entered the courtroom the first day of the trial, we saw that all the seats were already taken by KGB agents, militiamen in mufti, and several women wearing heavy makeup. Witnesses, friends and acquaintances of the priest, only a small number of whom gained access to the courtroom, had to stand throughout the trial.

The trial lasted from 9:00 AM until 6:00 PM. Among the witnesses were some elderly mothers of large families, exhausted by communal farm work, including one mother of four recuperating from abdominal surgery, and also one war veteran missing a leg. When I suggested to the young men who were seated that they should allow the tired mothers and invalids to have a seat, they angrily retorted, "If they're tired, let them get out . . . nobody is keeping them here. . . ." The poor men did not understand that all those people had been brought here and were being kept here by love and respect for the priest. Bored, they paged through newspapers and talked among themselves, paying no attention to the trial, while cynically ridiculing the faithful who were saddened and concerned about the priest's fate.

Summoned to the trial as witnesses were about seventeen children, ages seven to ten, and their parents. Even before the trial, the children were threatened by the principle of the Dubingiai Primary School and several chekists.[1] Pushing and even striking the children, they pressured them to sign edited statements alleging that "in the church hall the priest taught children religion." Of the seventeen, only four signed, but even these four stated during the trial that they had signed under duress, not even knowing the contents of the statement.

All the witnesses, including the children, were isolated from one another until their appearance on the stand. The officials intimidated and threatened the children and the parents in all sorts of ways, demanding that they testify that the priest had taught the children religion. However, the parents all testified that they themselves, or close relatives, had taught the children

---

[1]Chekist—another name for a KGB agent, from *Cheka*, the former name of the KGB.

religion, and the priest had only tested their knowledge. Therefore, they asked that they, the parents, be sent to prison, and
not the priest. However, no one paid attention to them.

Summoning the child witnesses one by one, the judge told
them, "It is good that you studied religion. It is necessary to
study. I studied myself. After all, the priest taught you, didn't
he?" The children were very frightened, many of them wept,
but all of them replied that it was not the priest who had taught
them, but rather their mother, father or grandmother.

After the trial, the four children became seriously ill.
Feverish, weeping and restless, they shouted that they were
afraid of the militiamen.

After the first day of the trial, Father Seskevicius offered
the Holy Sacrifice of the Mass in the evening, with weeping
parishioners participating. During the sermon, he asked all of
the faithful to respond to hatred and injustice with love and
prayer, according to the example of the crucified Jesus Christ.
Kneeling at the foot of the cross, the children thanked God for
helping them not to be afraid of the officials' threats and to tell
the entire truth in court.

The second day of the trial even fewer people were allowed into the courtroom, and only officials were given seats.
They abrogated the priest's right to present witnesses. Hardly
had the court recessed when two militiamen burst in and, without explanation, escorted the only witness present out of the
courtroom. Immediately afterwards, the Assistant Chief of the
Moletai Militia, Tamosiunas, entered the room. chekist agents
standing at the door pointed at me and said, "Grab her!"

Tamosiunas seized me by the hand, which I disengaged,
but two militiamen sprang forward, twisted my arms behind my
back, and took me from the courtroom. They seated two of us
in an automobile, and Tamosiunas drove us to a militia station.
The militiamen joked that it had been planned ahead of time to
escort two of us roughly from the courtroom, in order to
frighten all the others.

The other woman detained was the mother of four children; she had recently undergone abdominal surgery and her third daughter, little Therese, after being frightened the day before in court, was very ill. I explained all of this to the chief of militia and asked him to release her since he knew what sort of "offenders" we were. He mocked me, but a half hour later, he put the woman on a bus to her collective farm, ordering the driver not to let her off along the way, lest she return to the trial. The woman was very pale, and weeping from fright.

After the trial was over, and the priest had been taken off to the Lukiskiai Prison in Vilnius, Tamosiunas returned to the militia headquarters and bragged to me, "We sentenced the priest!" He had received one year of hard labor, and Tamosiunas explained that they had detained me because they wanted peace and quiet in the courtroom. Yet in the courtroom, no one had caused a disturbance, and the judge had not warned me once.

When Tamosiunas began to make fun of the Faith, I told him that you cannot make fun of something with which you are not familiar. Tamosiunas replied, "You are well read on the subject of religion, but Ragauskas was smarter than you. Have you read what he has written?"

"Yes, I have read his books, but before death, he regretted that he had written so and called for a priest, but two chekists guarded the entrance to his ward and would not allow any visitors in. The hospital personnel heard how he prayed out loud, reciting the *Miserere* and other penitential psalms."

Tamosiunas was surprised, and after a moment of thought said, "Ragauskas prayed before dying because he had become senile."

Surprised, I asked, "Just a few months before Ragauskas' death, an article was printed in the republic newspaper under his by-line. They don't print articles by senile writers, do they? Ragauskas was only sixty. He was suffering from abdominal cancer and could not have become senile in two months after writing the article."

Tamosiunas did not answer, but changed the subject. Thus, he was the first of the government atheists to bear witness publicly (in the presence of all those militiamen) that the ex-priest Jonas Ragauskas had prayed before his death. May the Lord have mercy on his soul.

After that, Tamosiunas returned my purse and internal passport, which he had taken when he was escorting me from the courtroom, first making a notation from the passport for the Vilnius KGB. I was already preparing to leave, when suddenly the door opened and the Chief of the Moletai KGB, intoxicated, stumbled into the room. Seeing me, he lurched nearer and banging his fist on the table, shouted, "Why have you come here? What do you want here? Why are you defending him? What is he to you? Do you know that he has blood on his hands?"

His anger was so great that as he shouted, his spittle flew in all directions. The militiamen who had been in the room slunk off to the side. I calmly explained to him that my late mother and Father Seskevicius had been students together at the Birzai High School, so she knew him well, and always respected him. And I also respect all priests.

He went on shouting that he knew everything about me, that he had recordings of my conversations with the priest, and so on.

"I'm not the least bit interested in what you have," I replied. After a while, when I continued answering him calmly, the KGB chief quieted down. But it was midnight before they released me from the militia station.

For the first time, I felt how unfortunate are those who do not have faith or love. I saw how the suffering of Father Seskevicius—his imprisonment—accepted with love, touched their hearts and consciences. Would that more people could be found determined to go to Golgotha with Christ and to die with Him.

Harassment and Arrest

Very soon after the trial, I was summoned to the Vilnius KGB, where chekist Gudas and chekist Kolgov reprimanded me for daring to engage an attorney for Father Seskevicius. Gudas threatened to throw me out of work, to take away my co-operative apartment, to expel me from Vilnius, and to "take care of" my brother Jonas Sadunas. When I refused to be intimidated, Gudas began shouting, "We'll bring a case against you, like the one against Seskevicius, and you'll go to prison with him!"

I replied that I gladly agreed to suffer for the truth. At this, Gudas could not restrain himself and slamming the door, he stamped out of the office. Convinced that I had not been intimidated by their threats, they released me, but from that time on, they followed me at every step.

I noticed this only during the summer of 1974, prior to my arrest. It seemed that two or three KGB agents were following me everywhere. Accordingly, I prepared myself for a raid by destroying or hiding everything that in the event of my arrest could cause unpleasantness for others—letters written to me, addresses, peoples' work or home telephone numbers, etc.

On August 27, 1974, after praying in the chapel of the Mother of Mercy of the Dawn Gates, I came home with number 11 of the *Chronicle of the Catholic Church in Lithuania*,[2] planning to copy it. Along with it I brought home the small typewriter which the late Canon Petras Rauda had given me. As I entered my apartment at Architektu 27-2, I met my brother on his way to the Polyclinic. I did not have a chance to speak with him.

In my room about 2:00 p.m., I began copying the *Chronicle*. Hearing me, a neighbor woman, a teacher named Mrs. Aidietiene, who was an informer I did not suspect at the time, called the KGB and told them I was typing. (Chekist Vytautas Pilelis mentioned this to me during my interrogation: "You sympathize with everyone, but no one sympathizes with you. You had hardly started typing the *Chronicle* when the woman next door immediately informed us of the fact, by telephone." I replied, "If she did so convinced that she was doing right, I respect her. And if she did it for spite, I am sorry for her.")

When the chekists came and surrounded the house, that same neighbor hurried at their orders to the Polyclinic to find out whether my brother would be returning home soon, since the chekists had decided to enter the apartment at the same time as he, and so to surprise me while I was typing. And that is exactly what they did. About 4:00 as soon as my brother returned, a whole group of chekists tumbled into our apartment. Three of them opened the door to my room, and saw me sitting at the typewriter, talking with Brone Kibickaite, my best friend, who was sitting nearby, and they began shouting, "Don't move! Hands up!"

Smiling, I asked them, "Why are you shouting so? Have you seen an atom bomb?" I said this so calmly that Brone thought that some acquaintances of mine had come in and tried

---

[2]The *Chronicle* is an underground, periodical account of the Lithuanian Catholic struggle to survive under an atheistic and totalitarian regime. It is circulated through the diligent efforts of those in the resistance, who type multiple copies for private distribution. Word processors and copying machines are unknown in such circles.

to frighten her. She asked them, "And how did you get here?"

They did not answer her, but only stated that they had a search warrant and were going to use it. They advised me to surrender anything incriminating. I stood up and said, "The thing you are most interested in is the *Chronicle of the Catholic Church in Lithuania*. Here it is. You won't find anything else here."[3]

"Sit down at the typewriter!" the chekists shouted. "We want to photograph you."

"If you want a photograph, sit down yourselves," I replied, and moved away.

They told Brone and me to stand in the corner and not to move about. They started to search, and we two, in order not to waste time, began praying the rosary aloud, saying, "You go on about your work while we pray."

The poor chekists felt very uncomfortable, because instead of being afraid of them, we calmly prayed. In the middle of the search, the chekists took Brone Kibickaite, and carried out a search of her apartment (Tiesos 11, apartment 38) but they found nothing "illegal". Still later, they took my brother to the KGB office, so that they could later carry out a search of his room without him, without me and without a warrant, completely ignoring my strong protest against the terrorizing of my

---

[3]According to the *Chronicle of the Catholic Church in Lithuania* (No. 28, June 29, 1977), one of the KGB agents said to Nijole: "You are a Catholic. How can you type the *Chronicle of the Catholic Church in Lithuania*, which contains only lies and slander about the so-called persecution of believers?" She replied: "The accuracy of every atheist misdeed revealed in the *Chronicle of the Catholic Church in Lithuania* is confirmed by the tears of the faithful."

The agents also maintained that the article on the funeral of the late Canon Petras Rauda had probably been written by Nijole. She denied this allegation, saying that if she had written it, she would have included many more details about the harassment by KGB agents during the funeral. Later, as the chekists began to ridicule the late Canon Rauda, Nijole was outraged: "All of you together are not worth a single toe of Canon Rauda!"

sick brother. Chekists can get away with anything.

During the raid, the chekists seized three different issues of the *Chronicle*. Later, they took anything they wanted, without showing it to me, or entering it into the search report. In this way, my notes with thoughts on religious topics, photographs and other papers disappeared. But addresses of my friends and correspondents were well hidden, and they did not find them.

Suddenly one of the chekists began rejoicing that he had found some letters I had written. "Letters!" he shouted. I jumped up to him suddenly and grabbing the letters from his hands, I tore them into bits, while the chekist shouted, "Give them back!" I quickly ran to the hallway toilet next door and with a resounding flush, sent everything down the sewer. The chekists had not expected such sudden action on my part, and when they realized what was happening, it was too late. In this way people who had written to me were saved from interrogations and perhaps searches.

When they came to their senses, the chekists surrounded me shouting that they would take me away to the KGB headquarters and finish the search themselves. "You can take me," I said, "I am satisfied now that no one will suffer on account of me." However, they did not take me away and the search continued to the end. Into the room came chekist Kolgov, who smugly stated, "Four years ago we warned you. Since then we have been following your every step. . . . You did not mend your ways. Now you're going to get it. . . ."

"According to the Russian proverb," I told him, "one waits three years for a promise to be fulfilled. But I wait four years for you to put me in prison. You're late!"[4]

Kolgov became confused and began denying that they had ever promised me anything, claiming that I was imagining things.

---

[4]Nijole was charged with violating paragraph 68 of the Criminal Code of the Lithuanian SSR—anti-Soviet agitation and propaganda.

"It's good," I said, "that you have warned me in time with whom I am dealing. Now I will not speak with you at all, lest I 'dream something up again'." Thus was born my firm resolve not to speak with those slaves of falsehood, the chekists, about any aspect of the case during interrogation.

After the search, three chekists accompanied me to KGB headquarters, and the others, remaining behind in my apartment, carried out the search of my brother's room, without finding anything "illegal". Meanwhile Lieutenant Colonel Petruskevicius, who had led the raid, began interrogating me. In response to his question, "Where did you obtain the *Chronicle*," I replied, "I'm not going to answer any questions concerning the case because you yourselves are the criminals, crudely transgressing the most elementary rights of the faithful guaranteed by the Constitution, the Declaration of Human Rights, and by statute. So I express my protest against the case. I will not assist criminals in the commission of a crime!"

"For that, we'll shut you up in a psychiatric hospital," threatened Petruskevicius. "There it will be a hundred times worse than prison." But I did not become frightened, and he promised to let me go if I told him from whom I obtained the *Chronicle*. I kept silent.

In this way chekists are always breaking the law during investigations, and all of them should be brought to criminal trial according to Par. 187 of the Criminal Code: "The use of force by a person carrying out a search or preliminary investigation to compel one to testify, or forcing one to give testimony during a trial, by using threats or other unjust actions, is punishable by deprivation of freedom for up to three years. The same holds in connection with the use of deceit and with ridiculing a person under interrogation—punishable by deprivation of freedom for three to eight years."

However, this is only on paper while in reality, during the entire occupation of Lithuania, the chekists have deliberately broken this law, and not one has ever been brought to criminal trial, since everything is based on lies and deceit.

Failing to get anything out of me during interrogation, chekist Petruskevicius ordered the soldiers to take me down to the KGB cellar—to solitary confinement. A woman came in, searched me, taking away everything, even the cross from around my neck, my rosary and a medal. Afterwards, they took me to a separate corner cell where they kept me about seventeen days.

Interrogation:
The Cellars of the KGB

In the cellars of the KGB—the interrogation solitary section—the old methods of torture used during interrogations as described in the *Gulag Archipelago* have been changed for a new kind. In the KGB cellars are hot cells and cold cells. They kept me, Vladas Lapienis, Father Alfonsas Svarinskas (1983) and many others in hot cells where one is constantly being stifled from lack of air and from heat, perspiring ceaselessly.

On the other hand, Genovaite Navickaite, Ona Vitkauskaite and others were kept in cold damp cells with water dripping from the walls. There it was so cold that they were frozen to the marrow, and their joints ached. Moreover, they felt so weak that they could hardly walk. They suffered from severe and unexplainable headaches and stomach cramps, and when they lay down, they lacked the strength not only to get up, but even to move a hand. Only after some time would they gradually recover.

Vladas Lapienis was kept for a long time in a cell where his whole body began aching. When he scratched himself in his sleep, festering sores would appear. He began having heavy nosebleeds, and to feel severe anxiety, fear of the door being opened, etc. When he became extremely weak and asked during interrogation whether, upon his death, his remains would be turned over to his wife for burial, the chekists took him to another cell, where all these problems vanished.

Vladas Lapienis suffered from hypertension, but after interrogations, and even now that he has returned from Siberia, his blood pressure is constantly very low. Only God knows what chekists use in their desire to break the will of those under interrogation. Moreover, they keep you all the time in a cell with a KGB informer, usually a criminal offender, who, when discovered, begins to rage and to harass you in every way.

The KGB cells are deep underground, and only the top of a small window at the ceiling reaches the ground outside—the pavement of the KGB yard. The little window is barred with double panes of filthy glass, and you can barely see a patch of sky. To reach that window, one must climb up on a small table, and this is strictly forbidden.

Those under interrogation are taken outside for a half hour of exercise daily (it is supposed to be forty-five minutes, but the soldiers cheat on the time) in the little yard, similar to a cement cave—with high cement walls and floor, and above bars with narrow apertures. The little yards are four by five paces, or a bit larger. All around are the high walls of the KGB headquarters. Throughout the interrogation period, one does not see a tree or a blade of grass.

In the corridor of the interrogation-isolation section, three military guards pace ceaselessly, and they are constantly looking into the cell through a small "eye" in the door. Among themselves they curse and swear, especially the most vile Russian profanity, cursing one's mother. When I complained to Major Pilelis about the cursing of the Communist Youth League soldiers, he told me with a smile that there was no harm; they do not know how to talk in any other way, and use profanity as a connective between words. Such is his Communist morality, to curse everything noble and sacred, and only when mingling with foreigners to don the deceiving mask of culture.

How sad that there are still people abroad who believe the lying promises, agreements and "good-will" of the Communists. The Communists promise much, in order to cause the lowering of one's guard, and later, to cause greater harm—to swallow a larger bite. All of the agreements and documents they sign are mere deception, immediately broken in the most cynical fashion. Every dialogue with Satan, or his willing slaves, is a crime. True love does not consist in helping them to do evil, or in believing in their lies, but rather, in boycotting evil. The Communists, like the serpent in the Garden of Eden, promise much, but bring death.

Even though it was very hot in the cell, and there was no ventilation, my morale remained good because they had taken me alone and I had not involved anyone else. In thanksgiving to God, I sang hymns, and the guards banged on the cell door, shouting for me to be quiet. Because I would not obey them, they wrote me up in a report to the chief of the isolation section, and personally complained, "They've brought us a long-playing record, and there's no way to stop it."

Soon after, I began losing hair dramatically, and losing weight. The KGB has ways of wearing down those under interrogation, with the idea that as one is physically weakened, the will is also weakened. But they do not know that even the weakest person, supported by Christ, is unbreakable.

Petruskevicius interrogated me for about two months, and when he could not get me to talk, he gave up on my case. He also threatened me constantly with the psychiatric hospital, and he ridiculed all believers—"You are cowards! As soon as you wind up with us, you all head like rabbits for the bushes—You keep quiet, you don't answer questions, you give no testimony. Revolutionaries used to make the courtroom their tribunal. They used to speak the truth to your face. But you are cowards. . . ."

"Don't laugh at believers," I advised him. "You had better pick up the Scriptures and read the passage about David's battle with Goliath. It is most apt for the present situation. You, the KGB, are symbolically that Goliath today. Thousands of staff persons, hundreds of thousands of agents and informers—you have all the best means of detection and eavesdropping; in your control is all the power: the army, the militia, the prisons, psychiatric hospitals. As for deceiving the people, you have had special training in that and twenty years of practical experience, while we believers, weaker than little David, not only lack a slingshot and a stone, but you have even pulled the little crosses from our necks.

"Nevertheless, we, just like the little David, go up against you in the name of the Lord of Hosts, and if the good God wishes, we will have our day in court. Just wait a little. . . ."

And the good God did bless us. Despite the secrecy of my trial (only a few chekists were present) my words during the trial very quickly became known world-wide. "If God is with us, who can be against us?" He chooses the weak things of the world to shame those who think they are something. To Him alone be glory, thanks and love for all ages!

But this was in the future. For the present, Rimkus struggled with me for about two months, and not getting anything out of me, turned me over to the Assistant Chief, Kazys, of the Interrogation Section.[5] The very first day, when chekist Kazys

---

[5]According to the *Chronicle*, No. 28: "The interrogators [also] questioned many witnesses. Nijole's relatives were summoned, as were her acquaintances, but they still found no evidence against her.

At the beginning of 1975, the KGB intercepted a letter from Poland addressed to Nijole. Henrik Lacwik was not aware that she had been arrested. In his letter to Nijole, he wrote about his 1974 stay in Lithuania. In February, 1975, the KGB agent Platinskas travelled to Poland to see Lacwik. The KGB agent asked about his visit to Lithuania, and also whether Nijole had spoken about the *Chronicle of the Catholic Church in Lithuania*, persecution of the priests or believers in Lithuania, and whether she had given him any reading material. The replies were negative.

The KGB was aided by Nijole's cousin, Vladas Sadunas, and . . . on March 25, 1975, Regina Saduniene (wife of Vladas Sadunas) took issue

received no answer to a question in connection with the case, he began shouting, "You schizophrenic!"

"It seems as though you are not only the interrogator, but also a psychiatric genius," I told him in surprise. "You've hardly even seen me, and you are so firm in your diagnosis. . . ."

"Yes, I am a psychiatrist," Kazys confirmed, "and when they take someone to the crazy house, I am the first to sign."

"To my knowledge, schizophrenics are most often victims of a disease of megalomania. Since you consider yourself to be a genius, it would be best for you to take care of your health," I advised him. Kazys blanched from anger and began pacing about the office. After that he began to threaten and intimidate, and even to show me pictures of Lithuanian partisans which had absolutely nothing to do with my case.

They questioned me the entire day, and when a soldier escorted me in the evening to the KGB cellar—my prison—I requested paper and wrote a protest to the prosecutor, with copies to the chief of the KGB and to the chief of the interrogation section.

In my statement, I protested against the hooliganism which the chekists Lieutenant Colonel Petruskevicius, Major Rimkus and Kazys engage in during interrogations. They force people to make statements by threatening confinement in the psychiatric hospital. In my petition, I emphasized that I was not opposed to psychiatric expertise, but only against the chekists' constant ridiculing of human dignity. I said that it would be better for them to beat me, because physical wounds heal more quickly than moral traumata. I refused to go for interrogation unless the investigators put a stop to this hooliganism.

For about two weeks, they did not take me for interrogation, and after that I received from the KGB Prosecutor, Baku-

---

No. 8 of the *Chronicle of the Catholic Church in Lithuania* to KGB headquarters, although at the trial she would testify that she had found the said issue on her husband's desk, but did not know where it came from. Nijole had not given her anything to read.

cionis, the following reply: "Investigators have the right to make psychological tests, but in this case they see no need."

Kazys interrogated me just one day. After Bakucionis' reply to my protest, the much-touted chekist, Vytautas Pilelis, began interrogating me. When the soldier took me to the interrogation, Pilelis asked, "So you're complaining, are you?"

"I am not complaining, but protesting," I answered.

"You see," said the chekist, "I have been working here for over twenty years. I've seen all sorts of iron men during that time . . . for a week or two, they would maintain some spirit, but after that all their chins were dragging on the ground. But it's already the fifth month that you, under these conditions, have been walking around from morning till evening, smiling. We've never seen anybody like you."

"It was not on account of my good spirits that your chekist colleagues have threatened me with confinement in the psychiatric hospital, but because I won't make statements for them," I interrupted Pilelis.

"So, if you would give us just one statement, we would let you go home," Pilelis deceitfully promised.

"If you gave me eternal youth and and all the beautiful things in the world for one statement which would cause some trouble, then those years would turn into hell for me. Even if you kept me in the psychiatric hospital all my life, as long as I knew that no one had suffered on my account, I would go around smiling. A clear conscience is more precious than liberty or life. I do not understand how you, whose conscience is burdened by the spilled blood and tears of so many innocent people, can sleep at night. I would agree to die a thousand times rather than be free for one second with your conscience!"

Major Pilelis blanched, and hung his head. Momentarily, he seemed petrified. I understood that he recognized the depths of his depravity, but lacked the strength, or perhaps, the will, to rise from that quagmire. (On my return from Siberia, I found out that Pilelis' past is truly terrible.)

After some time, the poor chekist picked up his head and angrily threatened, "If that's how it is, then we'll kick you out of here right now, and using your name we'll carry out raids and arrests as though you did betray people. (Here, he named a whole list of the best people.) It would be nothing for us to forge your signature under the records. So you see, your friends will turn their backs on you as a traitor, and we won't give you the time of day."

"You frighten me," I smiled. "Let everyone turn away from me. I don't need people's approval. The only thing I need is a clear conscience. As for your time of day, keep it!"

"We know everything now, anyhow," Pilelis persisted.

"If you know everything, then why are you questioning me?" I asked him.

"Not everything," he hedged, "but a lot."

To intimidate me, he began to tell me, "On such and such a day, at such and such a time, so and so (all accurate) came to see you, and you served them a prune compote." I felt uneasy, not wishing to implicate innocent people. Mentally, I prayed to God to help me, when I suddenly remembered a very humorous incident which had just happened in the cell, and burst out in the most spontaneous laughter.

Pilelis had expected anything but this laugh of mine. He was so distracted and confused that he fell silent, gaping, and looked at me very surprised for a few minutes. He knew that what he had been telling me caused me no laughter. He must have thought that I was acquainted with the legal nicety that whatever the chekists discover in snooping around has no legal value until people themselves, frightened by the chekists' knowledge, admit it. But in reality, I did not know that. From that time on, for the next six months of interrogation, Pilelis did not once mention what they had discovered in spying on me.

One day, he began to praise me profusely, "Throughout my career, I have never met anyone like you, who has done so much good for people."

I asked why he was praising me so highly.

"It's not flattery, but the truth," said the chekist.

"And in spite of the fact that I have really tried to do only good for everyone," I said to him, "at my trial, you are going to give me a greater sentence than you do murderers."

"Yes, you are going to get more than murderers, because you know too much," affirmed Pilelis.

The next day, he called me and other believers who had been arrested—the late Father Virgilijus Jaugelis and Petras Plumpa—fanatics. "That appellation fits you, yourselves, best," I told him, "because you try with all your might to make us atheists, but believers love all people because Jesus Christ said, 'What you do for anyone, you do for me.' We fight only against evil. For you we feel sorry, and if necessary, we would give our lives for you. You know that!"

Yes, Pilelis knew it, but in spite of that, he wrote in the space specially left in the witnesses' depositions, after they had signed them and departed, that they had testified that I was a fanatic. I saw that falsification when I looked over the case against me before the trial. On my return from Siberia, I asked those witnesses whether they had said I was a fanatic. Not one of them had said so, and some of them did not even know the meaning of the word. The chekists charge everyone who is on trial for religion with religious fanaticism. From this it is clear that there are secret instructions from Moscow to this effect.

One time, when a soldier brought me for interrogation, there were two other chekists in the office with Pilelis. This used to happen often, because Pilelis mentioned that he is afraid of me, since during the raid I had been able to destroy letters in front of a dozen chekists. "I don't know what she might do," he has said. So we were rarely alone in the office.

In the presence of the two chekists, Pilelis stated, "You believers are never satisfied: If it's not one thing, its another. Do you think you would have fared better under the fascists?"

"I don't know what would have happened to us under the

fascists," I replied, "But I do know that you are worse than the fascists."

Pilelis jumped up and shouted, "What, we are worse than the fascists?"

"Yes," I replied. "The fascists committed a great crime, but they did not hide it. They stated openly whom they destroyed, whom they intended to enslave, and everyone knew about it. You commit the same crime, but disguised as 'liberators' and 'brothers', while behind your backs you hold that same bloody knife. What could be worse in a human being than hypocrisy! Since you are hypocrites, you are worse than fascists!"

"I'm going to put that in the record!" shouted Pilelis, snatching the piece of paper from the table.

"Write it down," I calmly told him, "I will repeat everything for you, word for word, and sign the deposition."

Pilelis, however, did not have enough nerve to enter my statement in the record, and he did not write a word of it.

During the tenth month of my interrogation, Pilelis showed me a picture of myself and asked what I could say about it. I was seeing the postcard-size picture of myself for the first time, and I understood that they had enlarged it from a small passport photograph which they had found during the raid.

In order not to implicate new individuals, I said, "If this has nothing to do with my case, and you do not take down my statements, I will tell you what I know about this photograph."

Pilelis assured me, "I give you the word of an investigator that this has nothing to do with your case, and I will not enter it into the record."

I told him that I was seeing my picture in this size for the first time, that someone had enlarged it from a passport photograph, reproduced it, and distributed it, so that people who did not know me could have that picture. But when I finished speaking, the chekist began entering everything in the record. "What happened to your word?" I asked him. Pilelis, smiling sardonically, said, "That's called legal astuteness!"

"If you consider lying legal astuteness, then as a sign of protest, I am not going to speak to you at all, from this moment on." I remained silent two weeks.

Two or three chekists and Prosecutor Bakucionis would come to the interrogation sessions and try to get me to talk, but since I remained absolutely silent, after two weeks they closed the case. Pilelis had ridiculed me the whole time, for not knowing anything, and for not being acquainted with the legal niceties, and when he finished interrogating me, he hissed through his teeth, "Well, aren't you tough!" When they closed the case, I breathed easier. "Thank God, the terrorizing of witnesses has ended!" Chekists Gudas and Vincas Platinskas contributed, but Pilelis especially. Vincas Platinskas terrorized Brone Kibickaite, even when he met her on the street: "Your place is with Nijole, in prison!"

Friends and relatives left in freedom always suffer more pain and worry than the prisoner. Since I had refused an attorney, I acquainted myself with the brief against me. Of the many witnesses questioned (on the matters reported in the three issues of the *Chronicle*), in spite of the chekist threats, everyone testified that the reports were true, but on June 16-17, they tried me for "libel", without having a single witness.

The Trial and the Defense

I was escorted to the trial by six soldiers, while even murderers are guarded by only one or two soldiers. They were des-
perately afraid lest my defense speech and my final statement
get out to the public.

At the beginning of the trial, Prosecutor Bakucionis, holding in his hand an envelope containing my defense speech and
my final statement (which I had not been able to smuggle out of
the KGB cellar) triumphantly exclaimed, "Don't say what you
are prepared to say today, and you'll go home from the trial
free!"

The Prosecutor in the Supreme Court offered me freedom
in exchange for my silence. How much they feared the truth! I
replied, "I am not a speculator, and I refuse to speculate with
my convictions. I will speak today!"

The Prosecutor blanched, and hanging his head, sat down.

Sitting in the courtroom were only six chekists; I was
guarded by young Russian soldiers who did not understand a
word of Lithuanian, hand-picked so that they would not understand what I had said in court.

I asked the judge why the courtroom was empty. He deceitfully affirmed that the trial was secret.[6]

"And why do you chase witnesses out immediately after their testimony? After all, even in a secret trial, they are supposed to remain until the end. I demand that they remain in the courtroom, because I need them."

The judge angrily shouted that neither he nor I were in charge, and that we all had to obey the law.

Then the judge threatened, "One more word, and we'll take you away! We'll sentence you *in absentia!*"

"You can take me away," I assented. "Then your trial will be triply unjust: without spectators, without witnesses, and without me, what kind of trial will that be?"

They allowed me to remain in the courtroom, to their extreme regret. When I began my defense speech, the prosecutor,

---

[6]An excerpt from the *Chronicle*, July 4, 1975, No. 17: "The Supreme Court of the Lithuanian SSR began considering the case of Nijole Sadunaite on July 16, 1975. The session began at 10:00 AM. It was chaired by Kudiriashov; the state Prosecutor was Bakucionis.

"The following witnesses were summoned to appear: Jonas Sadunas (Nijole's brother), Vladas Sadunas (her cousin), Regina Saduniene (Vladas' wife), Povilaitis (the principle of the middle school), Kusleika and Brone Kibickaite.

"At the start of the session the witnesses were isolated and were ordered out of the courtroom after giving their testimony, so they could not follow the court proceedings.

"Only six soldiers and five KGB agents were in the courtroom. The chief judge allowed only Jonas Sadunas, Nijole's brother, to remain; outsiders were not permitted to enter. KGB guards informed them that the court proceedings were closed."

Nijole refused to accept the services of an attorney, lest anyone get in trouble as she had for assisting Fr. Seskevicius at his trial; she also refused to answer the questions of the court. Of all the witnesses, only one testified that Nijole had given him copies of the *Chronicle of the Catholic Church in Lithuania*, and even he admitted later (while intoxicated) that he did so in fear of the KGB. Nijole protested several times against the judge's abuse of the law, whereupon the prosecutor recommended a sentence of four years at hard labor followed by five years in exile.

the judge and associate judges hung their heads and lowered their eyes:[7]

> I would like to tell you that I love all of you as my brothers and sisters and, if need be, without hesitation, would give my life for each of you. Today, that is not necessary. But I must tell you the sad truth to your face. It is said that only he who loves has the right to criticize and scold. In addressing you, I make use of the right. Each time people are tried in connection with the *Chronicle of the Catholic Church in Lithuania*, the following words of Putinas[8] seem most appropriate:

>> "In arrogant tribunals
>> Murderers condemn the just.
>> You trample altars,
>> Both sin and righteousness
>> Collapse under the weight
>>   of your statutes."

> You well know that the supporters of the *Chronicle of the Catholic Church in Lithuania* love their fellow man and are struggling only for their freedom and honor, as well as the right to enjoy freedom of conscience, which is guaranteed to all citizens without regard to their beliefs by the Constitution, the law and the Universal Declaration of Human Rights. They are seeking to ensure that these will not remain just beautiful words on paper nor lying propaganda, as at the present, but will really be put into practice. The words of the Constitution and the law are important even if they are not applied in real life and the all-pervasive discrimination against believers is sanctioned.
> *The Chronicle of the Catholic Church in Lithuania*, like a mirror, reflects the crimes atheists perpetrate against believers. Immortality is not captivated by its own loathsomeness; it is horrified by its own reflection in the mirror.

---

[7]Judge Kudiriashov and Prosecutor Bakucionis were aware of the content of Nijole's defense speech and, fearing lest Nijole's speech be heard by witnesses, cleared the courtroom and only allowed her brother to remain. (*Chronicle*, No. 28, June 29, 1977)

[8]Vincas Mykolaitis-Putinas, Lithuanian poet (1893-1967).

The mirror, however, does not lose its value. A thief steals money; you rob people by taking from them that which is of greatest value—loyalty to their own beliefs and the opportunity to pass that on to their children—the younger generation.

The fifth article of the Convention in the Area of Education[9] guarantees the right of parents to determine their children's morals and religious education according to their own beliefs. Nevertheless, Mrs. Rinkauskiene, a teacher interrogated in my case, states in the record that "Since there is a single Soviet school system, there is no need to confuse the children and teach them hypocrisy."

Who teaches children hypocrisy? Is it parents, who are guaranteed the right to raise their children according to their own beliefs or teachers like these? Parents and not teachers are for some reason blamed when children, whose parents have lost their authority through the influence of the school, go to the dogs.

In the record of her interrogation, Miss Keturakaite, a teacher at Klaipeda Middle school No. 10 states: "Since I am a history teacher, I have occasion to explain questions of religion to my students. In explaining the origins of Christianity and at the same time the myth of the origins of Christ. . . ."

How can Miss Keturakaite explain questions of religion which are outside her area of competence, when she is illiterate even in the area of history, since she still maintains the obsolete atheist lie that Christ is but a legend. Such illiterates educate the younger generation and use their authority as teachers to instill lies in the consciousness of their students.

The interrogators, Lieutenant Colonel Petruskevicius, Chief of the Interrogation Subsection Rimkus and Deputy Chief of the Interrogation Section Kazys, threatened many times to put me in a psychiatric hospital because I did not answer their questions, in spite of my explanation that my silence was a protest against this trial. Having tired of these threats, I wrote letters of complaint to the state prosecutor of the republic, to the chairman of the KGB and to the chief of the interrogation section, requesting that the latter

---

[9]An intentional convention signed by the USSR.

place the letter in the record of my case. The letter was not placed in the record. But Deputy State Prosecutor of the Republic Bakucionis, who is seated right here, replied in writing that they have that right to carry out a psychiatric examination, though in the opinion of the interrogators, there is no basis for one.

But you see, that was not the subject of the letter, which was a protest against the abuses of the interrogators who seek to intimidate the person being interrogated and to force him to violate his conscience. In my letter I wrote, and I quote: "Does an interrogator have the right to threaten the person being interrogated with confinement in a psychiatric institution or with psychiatric testing, when the person being interrogated refuses to violate his conscience and his beliefs?"

During my interrogation, Lieutenant Colonel Petruskevicius repeatedly threatened me with confinement in a psychiatric hospital, which would be much worse than a prison, simply because I didn't answer his questions. The first time he saw me, Deputy Chief of the Interrogation Section Kazys officiously diagnosed me as schizophrenic, as having schizophrenic ideas, and threatened to have me examined by the Psychiatric Commission of which he is a member. Major Rimkus, the chief of the Interrogation Subsection, repeatedly threatened me with a psychiatric examination when I did not answer his questions.

Is Soviet justice based solely on fear? If I am mentally ill, I should be treated, not threatened with illness. Is one at fault if one is ill? But even the interrogators are not convinced of that, since for the fifth month in a row, they are threatening me with commitment to a psychiatric institution in an effort to break my will. By such conduct the interrogators violate human dignity and I protest such actions toward me. By the use of force to elicit testimony, the interrogators violate Article 157 of the Criminal Code of the Lithuanian SSR.[10]

---

[10]"A person conducting an investigation or a preliminary interrogation, who during the course of the interrogation uses force, threats or other illegal means to obtain testimony is liable to three years in prison. Similar actions which include the use of force or the mockery of the person being interrogated, are punishable by from three to five

After I sent my protest, Rimkus, the Chief of the Interrogation Subsection, reproached me for complaining and mocked me, saying: "If you react that way you are abnormal. You don't know all of the legal technicalities."

Yes, I am unfamiliar not only with the technicalities, but also with the essence of the law, since I didn't study it. However, I know now that it is normal for Soviet prosecutors to lie and slander others, not only to the accused but to complete strangers. Such actions constitute spiritual hooliganism, which should be punished, since it takes longer for a spiritual trauma to heal than a physical one.

You are not concerned at all with correcting injustice. On the contrary, you tolerate and encourage it. As proof, we can note that witnesses questioned in my case, who were able to verify the facts published in the *Chronicle of the Catholic Church in Lithuania*, were first asked how the facts could have reached the editors of the *Chronicle*, to whom they had told the facts, who had heard them and the like.

What you fear is the truth. The interrogators didn't question or summon those who are filled with hatred for those who are of differing opinions, those who discharged Stase Jasiunaite, a teacher at the Kulautuva Middle School, for wearing a crucifix, and who mocked her in various ways and would not even hire her as the lowliest kitchen help.

The investigators did not summon Markevicius, the Chairman of the Executive Committee of the Council of Workers' Deputies of Panevezys, or Indriunas, the Chief of the Finance Department, who discharged Maryte Medisauskaite, secretary-typist with nine years experience, because she attended church.

Yet you always claim that religion is a citizen's private affair, and that all people have equal rights without regard to their beliefs. Your propaganda is beautiful, but the actual facts are ugly! The interrogators paid no attention to the crime committed by Kuprys, the principle of the grammar school at Naujoji Akmene, and the other members of the Education Department, in discharging a teacher who, while on a field trip to Kaunas with her stu-

years in prison."

dents, permitted them to make use of a toilet in the Kaunas park where Romas Kalanta immolated himself. What a crime! It is strange that you are still frightened of the ghost of Romas Kalanta, but how is the teacher to blame?

The interrogators did not warn any of the senior physicians, who abuse their positions by not permitting the dying to avail themselves of the services of a priest, even when such services are requested by the parents themselves, or their relatives. Even a criminal's last wish is heard. But you have the nerve to mock a person's most sacred beliefs, at one of his most trying moments—the hour of his death—and like thieves you brutally rob thousands of believers of their moral rights. That is your Communist morality and ethics!

Angus, an instructor at the University of Vilnius, coarsely slandered Pope Paul VI, the late Bishop Pranciskus Bucys, Father George Laberge and Father Pranas Raciunas. When will that loathsome slander be retracted? It was not withdrawn because lies and slander are your daily bread.

Frightened by the ideas of Mindaugas Tamonis, an engineer working in the area of the restoration of monuments and a recipient of a candidate's degree in the technical sciences, you confined him to the psychiatric hospital on Vasaros Gatve, hoping to "cure" him of his beliefs.

Who gave you the right to tell the pastors which priests they may or may not invite to retreats or devotions? After all, the historic decree, *On the Separation of Church and State, and Church and School*, affirms that the state does not interfere in the internal affairs of religious groups. In Lithuania, the Church is not separated from the state, but is oppressed by it. Government organs interfere in the internal affairs of the Church and its canons in the coarsest and most unacceptable manner. They order priests around arbitrarily, and punish them with no regard for the law.

These and hundreds of other facts witness that the atheist purpose—to make everyone their spiritual slave—justifies any means: lies, slander and terror.

And you rejoice in your triumph? What remains after your triumphant victory? Moral ruin, millions of unborn fetuses, defiled moral values, weak debased people overcome by fear and with no passion for life? All of that is the fruit of your labors. Jesus Christ was correct when he said, "You shall know them by the fruits." Your crimes are propelling you to the garbage heap of history at an ever increasing speed.

Thank God not all people have been broken. Our strength in society is not in quantity but in quality. Fearing neither prison nor labor camp, we must condemn all actions which bring injustice and degradation, or which result in inequality or oppression. Every person has the sacred duty to struggle for human rights.

I am happy that I have had the honor to suffer for the *Chronicle of the Catholic Church in Lithuania*, which I am convinced is fair and necessary, and to which I will remain faithful until I breathe my last. Thus, pass what laws you like, but keep them yourselves. What is written by man must be distinguished from that which is ordained by God. What is due to Caesar is but the remains of that due to God. The most important thing in life is to free one's heart and mind from fear, since concessions to evil are a great crime.

They sat there, pale, not once raising their eyes, like criminals condemned to death. I wished that I could have photographed those faces. Poor men, they realized they were committing a crime! This was noticed even by the Russian soldiers, who asked me after the trial, "What kind of trial was this? For two years, we have been escorting those on trial, and we have never seen anything like it. You were the prosecutor, and all of them were like criminals condemned to death! What did you speak about during the trial to frighten them like that?"

The second day of the trial, during my final statement, those trying me also sat there pale, with their heads drooping. Here is what I said:

This is the happiest day of my life. I am being tried on account of the *Chronicle of the Catholic Church in Lithuania*, which is struggling against physical and spiritual human tyranny. That means I am being tried for the truth and the love of my fellow man. What can be more important in life than to love one's fellow man, his freedom and honor?

Love of one's fellow man is the greatest form of love, while the struggle for human rights is the most beautiful hymn of love. May this hymn forever resound in our hearts and never fall silent. I have been accorded the inevitable task, the honorable fate, not only to struggle for human rights, but also to be sentenced for them. My sentence will become my triumph! My only regret is that I have been given so little opportunity to work on behalf of my fellow man.

I will joyfully go into slavery for others and I agree to die so that others may live. Today, as I approach the Eternal Truth, Jesus Christ, I remember His fourth beatitude: "Blessed are they who thirst for justice, for they shall be satisfied."

How can one not rejoice when Almighty God has guaranteed that the light will conquer darkness and the truth will overcome error and falsehood! I agree not only to go to prison but to die, in order to hasten that end. I want to remind you of the words of the poet Lermontov[11]: "The justice of the Lord, however, is just." The Lord willing, God's justice will be favorable to us all. Throughout my life I will pray to the Lord for you, I wish to conclude by reading the following verses which came to me in prison:

> The harder the way I must traverse,
> The more I understand life.
> We are all obliged to strive for truth,
> Conquering evil, without regard to the
>   difficulty of the task.
> Our brief days on earth are not meant for rest,
> But to participate in the struggle for
>   the happiness of numerous hearts.
> Only he who fully participates in that struggle
> Will feel he is on the right road.
> One can experience no greater happiness
> Than the determination to die for others.
> On such occasions one's heart is filled with joy

---

[11]Lermontov, Mikhail Yurevich—Russian Poet (1814-1841).

Which cannot be ended by prisons,
or cold labor camps.

Thus let us love one another and we shall be happy.
He alone is unhappy who does not love. Yesterday, you
were surprised by my happy disposition at a hard moment
in my life. That proves the fact that my heart is filled with
love for my fellow man, since loving others makes everything else easy!

We must sternly condemn evil, but we must also love
our fellow man, even though he has erred. That can be
learned only in the school of Jesus Christ, who is the only
truth, way and life for all. Dear Jesus, Thy kingdom come
in our hearts!

I would like to request the court to free from prison,
labor camps and psychiatric hospitals all of those who
fought for human rights and justice. That would be a sig-
nificant contribution in the effort to spread harmony and
goodness in life, and would mean that the beautiful slogan.
"Man is brother to man," would become a reality.

On June 17, 1975, Judge Kudiriashov handed down the
court's decision: "For duplicating and disseminating the *Chronicle of the Catholic Church in Lithuania*, she is sentenced to three
years loss of freedom, to be served in strict regime labor camps,
and to three years of exile."[12]

-----

[12]After the trial, Interrogator Pilelis confided to Nijole, "Based on
the offense committed your sentence is too severe."

One patient wrote Nijole at the labor camp: "In our Soviet reality,
we are accustomed to give everything different names: Truth is lying;
good is evil; facts are slander. National heroes are wrongdoers or criminals."

The accuracy of these words is confirmed by the court's dealing
with Nijole Sadunaite. The case was grossly fabricated, even the witnesses (Povilaitis and Vladas Sadunas) were specially bribed and
coached by the KGB. For example, when drunk, Vladas Sadunas
admitted to relatives that the KGB had forced him to testify that
Nijole had given him several issues of the *Chronicle* and the book
Simas to read. The relatives asked why he had not explained this at
the trial. He apparently replied that the KGB would then have had
his head. (From the *Chronicle*, No. 28)

To the Labor Camp

After the court's decision, the prison's "black raven" (the prison vehicle sheeted in black iron) returned me to the KGB cellars, but this time, very briefly—for just a couple days. The day after the trial, they granted me a brief visit with my brother, Jonas Sadunas. Before the visit, a soldier herded me to a cell in solitary, where a female KGB medical aide stripped me and searched everything in detail. I was subjected to the same "medical procedure" after the visits, also.

My brother had brought me a dark red rose, which my KGB guards examined for a long time, looking over each leaf to see whether anything was hidden there. During the visit, they seated me and my brother carefully. We were separated by a glass partition and wide table, and the prison guard did not take his eyes off us the whole time, constantly interrupting our conversation, demanding that we speak only of meaningless, everyday topics. Otherwise, he threatened to cut the visit short.

After our visit, my brother wished to give me food and clothing for the journey to the Mordovia Concentration Camp, but they would not take anything from him. The chekists told him to bring them back the next day, and then they told him that I had already been taken away, even though this was a deliberate lie, for they took me away a day later. This is a standard torture—let them be hungry on the way!

Before taking me off to the concentration camp, on June 20, 1975, the same KGB female paramedic searched me in solitary confinement, while the soldiers searched my meager food and clothing reserves. They even tore the wrappers from candy, and seized all of my notes. Afterwards, having warned me, "say goodbye to Lithuania, you'll never see it again! You are in our hands, we'll do what we want with you!"—they took me in a "raven" to the Lukiskiai Prison in Vilnius.

There they shut me up in a concrete cubicle—a solitary confinement cell—where one can only sit surrounded by walls and facing the door. After sitting for a while, you begin to suffocate for lack of air, but this does not bother anyone. "You didn't come to a resort!" the guards taunt you.

After keeping me in that cubicle for several hours, the soldiers herded me into a "raven", already packed with criminal offenders. To isolate me from them, they pushed me into the raven's iron cubicle, a solitary confinement compartment like a steel coffin and drove us all to the Vilnius Railroad Station.

The "raven" is windowless; you see nothing, as if you were buried alive. In the Soviet Empire, a prisoner is not a person; he is treated somewhat worse than a beast. He is a slave without rights, despised and morally and physically abused non-stop by soldiers and guards.

After bringing us to the Vilnius Railroad Station, soldiers with dogs ordered us all from the "raven". Off on a siding, out of public view, the prisoner's railroad car awaited us. Lining us up, they positioned me first, as "an especially dangerous state criminal" (the Soviet term for prisoners of conscience), with four soldiers and two guards watching me. All the others—several score of male criminals—they lined up behind me, and guarded them with just a few soldiers and a couple of dogs. The prisoners were surprised, and asked where they had been keeping me, since I was so pale and exhausted, although they themselves did not look any better.

After ten months of living in the KGB underground prison, I saw again that the trees and grass were still green, that there was so much space about and the sky was so big, not at all like what is seen through a barred little window. What a joy to see all that! Thanks to the Creator for such beauty! Only there was no time for us to enjoy it all, because they quickly herded us into a railroad car.

In the prisoner's car, behind thick steel bars, are separate cubicles with steel-barred doors, fastened with a large lock. They locked me up alone in a cubicle made to accommodate two, while the male criminals were stuffed eight, or even twelve, to a four-place cubicle. At night, a wooden bench took the place of a bed. I was able to lie down on the bench, but the male prisoners, packed like herring in a barrel, had no room to lie down or to sit.

In the corridor, in front of our pens, paced three military guards. Before my pen, a soldier stood constantly with a rifle, never taking his eyes off me, lest I "evaporate". The guard was changed every three hours. The prisoners asked them what I had done, to be guarded so. They, most of whom were four-to six-time repeaters, had never seen anyone guarded so closely. They were surprised to learn that in the Soviet Empire there still are prisoners of conscience, and all of them cursed the Soviet government which, according to them, was alone responsible for their being dehumanized.

The soldiers shouted at us not to talk, that it was not allowed, but later even they got interested in the conversation. In the hearts of most of them there still flickered a spark of humanity, but it was covered over with hatred and the ashes of various kinds of evil—the result of atheistic upbringing.

On the trip, the prisoner is given one small loaf of black bread a day, very sour and under baked (they used to give us such bread in the KGB cellars and in the concentration camp, also—this bread is specially baked for prisoners), after eating which the stomach begins to ache as though a fire were burning, and a few small soggy and very salty little fish—herring—the size of a finger.

I used to refuse this ration, and would not eat it in order to avoid agony later, although when I was free, I had been able to eat everything and never experienced stomach trouble; I had been quite healthy.

Prisoners who ate the little herring would ask for water to quench their thirst, but the soldiers would make fun of them and purposely not give them anything to drink for hours on end, saying, "Let them suffer!" In the car, such an uproar and such cursing would begin, that it was sheer hell. When they had finally had their fun, the soldiers would bring a kettle of water. After drinking it, the prisoners would soon begin to ask to be allowed to go to the toilet. Once more the soldiers would torment the prisoners, purposely not taking them for several hours.

How much cruelty there is in the hearts of young soldiers eighteen to twenty years old! Almost all of them wore Communist Youth badges—"Lenin's grandchildren". They curse and swear as much as the worst criminals. So much for Communist morality!

Sometime after we had left Vilnius, we stopped, and our car remained at the siding for a whole day. No one gave us any food rations for the following day because it had not been foreseen that the journey to the prison at Pskov would take two days. The prisoners, weakened as they were, had to fast. After I pleaded with them for a long while, the soldiers agreed to distribute to the prisoners what I still had in the way of food, but it was nearly a drop in the ocean.

The transport is a special way of tormenting prisoners. The journey is specially drawn out to a month, or even two, when normally two or three days would be enough. The prisoner's cars are overcrowded. All of the prisoners almost ceaselessly smoke the worst grade of tobacco—*makhorka*—and the windows in the corridor of the car are not open during the day. The glass is opaque, so that people cannot see the pale prisoners being transported behind bars, but the car is so full of blue smoke that you cannot see anything a few paces away.

Anyone unaccustomed to smoking becomes dizzy as though poisoned. At night it is cold, because they open little windows. Most of the prisoners are very lightly dressed and the nights are often damp and cold even during the summer, to say nothing of winter.

Male political prisoners are transported in the same pen with criminals, who ridicule them, take away everything, and moreover beat them up. The soldiers just incite them and laugh, since prisoners of conscience are called fascists by the Soviets—such a one should be beaten!

Criminal prisoners have sunk to such depths of amorality that being in the same car with them, you feel the greatest moral suffering, to say nothing about those whose lot it is to be with them in the concentration camps. This has lately become, in the Soviet Union, a daily occurrence. The chekists now warn everyone, "We'll lock you up together with the criminals!" Or, "We'll shut you up in a psychiatric hospital!", or, "We'll hire murderers and they'll kill you tonight. And so there will be no trace of you left!"

On the way to the Female Political Prisoner Strict Regime Concentration Camp in Mordovia, I stayed four to six days in the jails of Pskov, Yaroslavl, Gorky, Ruzayev, and Potma—at transfer points. When, after a few days of travel, the soldiers would shove us out of the car, often kicking the weaker ones, and herd us into the "raven" which would take us to the jail, the "raven", covered in black sheet iron heated by the sun, and stuffed with prisoners, would be as hot as a furnace. People were suffocating. The thirst was agonizing. The limbs began to grow numb, for we were packed almost on top of one another—unable to move.

In a cubicle intended for one, they would lock me up with another female, and we would suffer together. The jails were also overcrowded. The cells held more than the allotted number of prisoners; hence it was necessary to wait and suffer almost a half-day in the "raven" until they would free a cell for the new arrivals.

They would let us out of the "raven" and into a common cell, from which, after a long delay, they summoned us, according to the paragraphs of the Criminal Code under which we had been sentenced, searched us, and assigned us to cells.

The jail cells are dismal, dirty and often full of a wide variety of parasites—bedbugs, fleas, lice, roaches—and in the little yards where they would take us a half-hour a day for exercise, there were rats.

In the cells, it is cold and damp, for no ray of sun gets in. In the windows are several rows of rusty bars. What is more, a perforated sheet of iron not only keeps the light from getting in, but even air. Hence in the cells the light burns day and night. At Pskov, they shut me up for a whole week in the jail's basement, in solitary. The ceiling of the cell was low, and the walls damp, with a concrete floor to which a rusty iron bed (without mattress) was fastened. Ushering me in, they issued an old, dirty and ragged blanket. Right in the cell was a hole in the floor for a toilet. The little window was sealed with sheet-iron, and the light burned all the time.

In the concentration camps and prisons, they feed you enough to keep you from starving: in the morning, in an iron bowl, are a few spoons of porridge, cooked from the lowest grade of groats, without any fat, and a cup of muddy water—tea. For lunch—a dipper of a thin concoction called *balanda*, and again, a few spoons of porridge, over which they poor some malodorous fat, or they give you a little piece of fish, from which the prisoners often get food poisoning. I, too, suffered food poisoning many times from that fare.

In the evening, once again, a few spoons of groats, and tea. They also give you half a little loaf of bread each day which, on account of its poor quality, I could not eat. For eating, they pass a *karmushka* through the opening of the door. It is strictly forbidden to speak to the prisoners distributing food. Often standing next to them are soldiers. All the prisoners are thin skeletons covered with pale, bluish skin. They often joke, "As long as the bones survive, the flesh will grow back."

When they took us from the jail, there would be another search, and again the "raven", the station, the iron bars in the railroad car; in my compartment now they would pack other female prisoners, and the journey continued.

Besides Pskov, we were temporarily incarcerated in the jails of Yaroslavl, Gorky, Ruzayev and Potma, where they would shut me up in the same cell with female criminals, including murderesses.

There were many female prisoners. I was with young fifteen-year old offenders sentenced for robbery and murder, with pregnant women, mature women and those who were quite old. I was amazed at the terrible amorality on the part of all of them, the complete loss of discernment between good and evil, the dehumanization. Here you see what a poor creature man is without God, and that the greatest offenders of all are those who systematically, forcibly and constantly infect everyone with the atheistic lie—the Soviet Government atheists. Those millions of poor dehumanized prisoners are the fruit of their "education".

Finally, they brought me to the last jail, in Potma, where they shut me up with female prisoners in a large cell. Instead of beds, as in the Gorky jail, we slept on slightly raised wooden pallets. We were attacked by bedbugs in such numbers that we began protesting. The guards told us that there were no bedbugs in the cell. Then we caught a few of them and, writing a protest to the warden, we included the bedbugs as evidence. After a half-day, they took us to another cell where there were fewer parasites.

In the prison yard and toilets, light brown rats roamed impudently (until then, I had seen only grey rats). After a few days, they herded us all into a train, but they did not put me in the same car with the female criminals. They told us that they had to transport "specially dangerous state criminals", namely me, in a separate compartment, under special guard. They shut me up alone in a double compartment.

The Potma prison guards were surprised that I did not know how to curse or swear. "Where did you come from?" they asked, "By the time they transport you from camp to exile, you will have learned everything." To their greatest surprise, their prophesy was not fulfilled—during my transport from camp to exile, I came to meet some of the guards again. I finally reached my last transfer point.

They shut me up in a separate cubicle in the railroad car and took me away. From Potma, a narrow-guage train transported the prisoners through swampy forests. Along the whole route, the only things we could see through the little open windows were barbed wire enclosures—concentration camps— soldiers, guards and dogs, one after the other, more than twenty concentration camps in which were crowded a whole Soviet republic of slaves. The hard-labor concentration camp for female political prisoners is reached after passing all the other concentration camps strung out along the railroad line, which carries prisoners almost exclusively. For this reason, they did not even close the little windows here. We had arrived in a slave state.

Finally we were at the last stop and they ordered us out. They sent various individuals to different places; I was herded into the reception room of the women's concentration camp, where I was searched. They took my copy of the court's decision for "verification", and they never returned it, even though I appealed to the concentration camp commandment many times in writing, asking him to return it. Soviet officials do not like to leave the decisions of their criminal trials with political prisoners, and they seize them from almost everyone soon after the trial, or after transport to camp. After the search, they put my clothing in storage, and clothed me in prison garb.

The journey from Vilnius to Mordovia had taken a whole

month.[13] The female prisoners greeted us with love and concern, and one Ukrainian prisoner gave me a pleasant surprise by laying out before my plate little flowers arranged in the form of the tricolor of independent Lithuania.

The women's concentration camp zone was small—a tiny triangular yard surrounded by a double fence of barbed wire and a third high fence of wood, so that one might not see anything. On top of this was a guardhouse. It was strictly forbidden for the prisoners to speak with guards.

In the center of the yard was a little old wooden house, or barrack, in which one room served as a dormitory, another as dining hall and next to it was the workroom where each prisoner was required to sew sixty pairs of work gloves a day. Anyone failing to fill her quota was taken to the punishment cell. The sewing machines were ancient, and would often break down. The thread was of poor quality and would snap every few minutes—sheer torture. I used to sew my quota from 6:00 AM to 11:00 PM with brief breaks for eating, exercise and prayer.[14]

---

[13]During the long and exhausting trip to Mordovia, Nijole lost thirty-three pounds. Camp food is very monotonous and of poor quality: barley mash without any fat, fish, left-over scraps of meat (cow udder, diaphragm, lungs). In the fall, cabbage soup is served for several months, but when the cabbage supply runs out, another kind of soup is made for several months, but always the same soup. Nijole fell ill on October 10, 1975, suffering from fever and dizziness throughout the Winter and on into the Spring of 1976. She was ill again the following Winter.

[14]Nijole's sufferings and strength of character are described more thoroughly in a letter written by her during this time: ". . . And how good it is that the small boat of our life is steered by the hand of a good Father. When He is at the wheel—nothing is frightening. Then, no matter how hard life becomes, you will know how to fight and how to love. And I can say that the year 1975 has flown by like the wink of an eye, but it has been my joy. I thank the good God for it. . . ."

"On March 3, I returned from the hospital. At last it looks as

It was good that we worked a whole day and there were not many of us. I would have been in the punishment cell constantly, because it is impossible to make one's quota during a single shift, with the sewing machine constantly breaking down.

The ceiling of the workroom was low, without any ventilators, so that the electric sewing machines would heat the place up. There was also a lot of dust, including dust from fiberglass with which we used to pad the palms of the gloves so that they would not wear out so easily. The gloves were intended for handling bricks, in construction and other work. Lately, they have raised the quota and the prisoner is supposed to make one hundred and ten pairs a day. The Soviets are unmerciful to their slaves!

Half of a prisoner's wages are deducted by the state to pay the salaries of the guards, KGB agents, etc., and from the remaining half, they take charges for food. For one month in a hard labor camp they take about twelve rubles. One can get some idea of the quality of the food, especially considering that the kitchen crew—female criminals cooked for us—used to steal prisoners' food and share it with the female guards.

They used to deduct for clothing, bedding, and so on. There was practically nothing left for the prisoner. If you filled your quota and had no "demerits", you were allowed to buy five

---

though I will be up and about, Your diagnosis was quite accurate—acute exhaustion.

"My 'vacation' lasted some time, I started it on October 18, [1975] and worked only six days in November, spent December in the hospital and only at the end of the month was I able to sew for four days. January I divided in half—one half I worked, the other half I did not. February was spent in the hospital; so were the first three days of March. Now I sew slowly, with pauses; when I feel weak I go outside into the yard to enjoy the fresh air and the sun. I fulfill my quota because we work only for one shift. . . . So for the time being, everything is going splendidly. Everyone loves me and I try to respond in kind. I am happy and satisfied." (Taken from the *Chronicle of the Catholic Church in Lithuania*, No. 23, June 13, 1976)

rubles worth of food, writing materials or soap per month at the concentration camp store. There was almost no food at the store, except for stale cookies, cheap candy, old preserves, tea and occasionally margarine, jam, oil and smokes of *makhorka*. Throughout my term, only a few times was there any white bread.

We were accompanied to the store by guards, and if there was money in our account which we had earned, we were allowed to buy; otherwise we could not buy. Money sent by friends and relatives could not be used for purchases—spending money had to be earned.

Prisoners who refused to perform compulsory labor sewing gloves or doing other work were punished during the whole term in the concentration camp: three consecutive fifteen-day stretches in solitary, followed by three or six months in a punishment cell, with brief respites between stretches. They were released to normal quarters for about a week, and everything began all over again. And so it went until the end of one's sentence. Utter invalids were excused from compulsory labor, but even those sick in bed were put to work assembling paper cartons.

When they brought me to the Mordovia Concentration Camp, there were twenty-one women prisoners confined there, and I became the twenty-second. Repairs were being made, and that week they allowed us to sleep in the yard on benches. What a pleasure when after a year in stuffy prison cellars, I could once more breathe fresh air and enjoy the starry sky! However, it only lasted a week, after which they herded all of us into the low and narrow dormitory where all of us had to sleep.

I slept on the second floor in the attic, until a bed became became available downstairs. There, it was a little easier to breathe, but oxygen was still in short supply because the windows were shut. It was too cold for the old prisoners, and the dormitory was not large; one bed next to another, with a nar-

row aisle down the center. Among the greatest physical sufferings were those concentration camp nights, when you longed for
the morning to be able to run out into the yard and get some
fresh air before work.

Because of the stuffiness, many suffered from insomnia,
yet by day, even the old were strictly forbidden to rest. Only
patients were allowed to lie down during the day; for the rest it
was a punishable offense.[15]

---

[15]Reflections from a letter written by Nijole particularly portray
her true character: ". . . I am grateful to those through whose efforts I
find myself here. I learned much and experienced much and all this
has been useful. After all, the good God knows best what I need. . . .

"In six days, it will be half a year since they took me from Vilnius,
but it all seems such a short time ago, as if it were yesterday. And
everything remains before my eyes—my 'honor' guard, sharers of my
fate, of whom there were many (they were all criminals, I was the
only political prisoner), the last farewell look at the city, or rather the
train station, and the whole 'romance' of the journey, which is
indescribable—it must be experienced in order to feel life and to
understand the necessity and the value of love. I have the possibility of
living through this romance a second time—when they take me into
exile. And you can only envy me for this, although that is not necessary—all this is not for people in your physical condition." (Taken
from the *Chronicle*, No. 23, June 13, 1976)

The Women in the Camp

> *"...There are many old women, as well as sick women here, so I am glad I was brought here according to my calling—to nurse and to love. And even though I miss you all very much, it will be difficult to leave here; I will be sorry to leave people who have become very close and dear to me. But then, the Good God cares best for us...."[16]*

The eldest woman in the Mordovia Concentration Camp was Tatyana Karpovna Kasnova, born in 1904. We used to call her "Baba Tanya" (Grandmother Tanya). A thin, petite little Orthodox woman, Baba Tanya was completely illiterate, able neither to read nor write.

How did she frighten Soviet government officials so badly that they sentenced her to seven years in the concentration camp and three years of exile as an especially dangerous criminal? Her whole "offense", like that of nine other Russian Orthodox women confined in the concentration camp, consisted of placing in people's mailboxes hand-copied verse, condemning the government atheists' ridicule and persecution of believers; in other words, she "libeled the Soviet government". Because So-

---

[16]From the *Chronicle*, No. 23, June 13, 1976.

viet officials oppose everything which is sacred to the believer, the woman openly used to call the Soviet government "the Satanic government" (*Sataninskaya vlast*).

Baba Tanya was particularly noted for her cleanliness, and like the other Orthodox women, she used to pray all day. They used to condemn the Orthodox hierarchy's criminal concessions to the government atheists and their cooperation with them, betraying the concerns of the faithful. Calling themselves the true Orthodox, the women used to keep a strict fast, abstaining completely from meat and animal fats; hence they usually ate only bread. Our porridge or soup often had a piece of scorched bacon or bacon bits thrown in it, so they would not eat such food, even though it contained barely enough fat for seasoning

We used to request the concentration camp administration not to have cooks put the bacon bits or fat in the kasha or soup being prepared for us, because the little Orthodox were forced to starve, and we ourselves often suffered food poisoning from the rancid fat. They would reply, "If you don't like it, don't eat it. You haven't come to a spa, you know." And they continued to prepare it as before.

When on May 1 (May Day) or November 7 (Anniversary of the Revolution), "the Devil's holidays" as the Orthodox women called them, they used to bring us a small roll as a supplement, not one Orthodox woman would take it. We began protesting against keeping such a woman as Baba Tanya in a strict labor camp. Never in the history of mankind has it been heard that a seventy-four-year-old, illiterate grandmother could be especially dangerous to the state!

Some sort of commission showed up and summoned Baba Tanya for an interview, but she told them that she did not need any favors from the representatives of the "Satanic government". They left her in the concentration camp until 1979, when they sent the seventy-five-year-old Tanya into exile.

The female prisoners in the transport took everything from her: her meager food reserves, clothing and even her little padded jacket. It was the end of October or the beginning of November, cold and damp. The difficult journey, lasting almost a month through various prisons, hunger and cold drained her completely of the last remnants of her poor health, and after she was brought to steppes of Kazakhstan, among complete strangers, on November 23, 1979, she surrendered her soul to the Lord. May she rest in Him!

Baba Tanya had my address with her, when I was still in exile in Siberia, and a good-hearted woman, at her request, wrote me a letter, in which she informed me that they had delivered Baba Tanya in seriously ill condition, and that shortly after her arrival on November 23, 1979, she had died. The militia immediately claimed her remains, and took them no one knows where. Baba Tanya died far from friends and relatives, her burial place is a mystery; but the sacrifice of her life has meaning. The deaths of martyrs are the brightest stars in the darkness of this life, a blessing in the Church Militant.

Earlier Baba Tanya had been in prison three years for her religion, under terrible conditions. They had kept her in a tightly-packed cell, without letting her out for exercise. All the women lay on a dirty cement floor, and used to receive a piece of bread and some water once a day.

A second Orthodox martyr was Irina Andreevna Kireeva, born 1912, who died in the concentration camp on May 26, 1980. Baba Ira, as we called her, was very kind and sensitive, always ready to help comfort the other women. She suffered from terminal cancer. For almost six months before her death, they kept her in the concentration camp hospital, where she became completely exhausted, but they would not let her go home. All of the female criminals, however, when they are incurable, are allowed to go home.

Baba Ira departed this life in the concentration camp, and her grave site also will never be known. They bury the remains of political prisoners secretly, merely tying on the hand the criminal case number which they write on a stake marking the burial place. There is no name—just the case number. The only ones allowed in those cemeteries are officials, chekists.

I was given this information by some of the soldiers who themselves had experienced much injustice and cruelty in the army, and who began to show us sympathy and even respect. Even though they used to be told that we were the worst kind of offenders, they wondered at the injustice, saying that the best people were locked up in the concentration camp, and the greatest criminals and moral perverts were in the commandants' jobs. This really is so.

Another Orthodox prisoner, Alexandra Akimovna Chvatkova, born 1906, was also very ill. Sentenced for the second time on account of her religion, she had spent much time in the punishment cell, because, like all the Orthodox women, she would not do forced labor in the concentration camp, in protest against her unjust sentence.

The long agonies, the cold and hunger, had undermined her strength. All her limbs ached, and often, her head; she had high blood pressure and was very pale and exhausted, suffering from cold constantly. With some other older women, she had made quilts from some old padded jackets which the guards quickly took away and burned, "Let them freeze, let them suffer, they didn't come to a resort!", they taunted as usual.

For covering, they used to give everyone a single, thin cotton blanket, like a thick sheet. We were all cold, for the nights in Mordovia are cool, even in summer; in the fall and spring, besides, it is damp; and in winter, there is the cold. However, they used to put up with all the sufferings very patiently, saying, "The harder, the better."

At the end of 1982, they transported Baba Yura Chvatkova to exile in Kazakhstan. I received no letter from her, since by that time I was in Vilnius, and almost all of my letters were confiscated by the KGB. Others wrote of her, and to this day, I do not have her address. May the good God help her and all not to give up in their love.

A fourth Orthodox prisoner, Klavdia Grigoryevna Volkova, was born in 1907. Baba Klava was very quiet and good. I slept in the bunk above her. The beds were double decker, made of iron, and very uncomfortable. When one rolled over, not only the upper bunk moved, but also the lower one, into which the upper is set; and conversely, when the prisoner in the lower bunk rolled over, the upper moved, awakening one constantly.

Baba Klava never used to complain when, suffocating at the ceiling for lack of air, I would flop around like a fish tossed ashore. She used to devote much time to fervent prayer. Sometimes all of the Orthodox women, gathered in some out-of-the-way corner, would quietly begin singing hymns. Once I learned them, I used to join in. I would feel as though I were in some shrine, such goodness and light would my soul experience.

Not without reason it is said that prayer in common reaches heaven. For several to pray together in the concentration camp is forbidden. The guards would often disperse us but we would gather again and again to praise and thank God for His love for us sinners. Common prayer—that used to be one of the brightest and happiest times in camp.

Only a year younger was yet another Orthodox prisoner, Anastasia Andreevna Volkova, who was born in 1908. The two Volkova's were not related, but both were sentenced together. Baba Nastia was a sick woman, with bad hands and feet, but very industrious; she was a good seamstress.

Since neither Volkova had been sentenced to exile, when they came out of concentration camp, they were both welcomed by good people in the City of Gorky. However, the "most humane" Soviet government did not leave these sick women in peace, and they were forced to go elsewhere.

A sixth Orthodox prisoner was Glafira Lavrentyevna Kulovsheva, born in 1924. When they arrested her, she left behind young daughters and a husband who was a Party member. He tempted her, saying that if she renounced her views, she would be released. She did not cave in. Then her husband renounced her, would not visit her and refused to help her, but instead, found himself another woman.

Glafira forgave everyone; she used to pray constantly, in tears, and she was very humble. She suffered from inflammation of the joints—polyarthritis. Even though she suffered greatly, she never complained, but would smile constantly and thank God for everything. After concentration camp, she suffered exile in Siberia for three years, and has now returned to her mother.

Among the younger prisoners was a woman in her forties, Tatyana Mikhailovna Sokolova, born in 1933. She was very quiet and friendly, yet suffered from diabetes, gastric disorders and massive headaches. In spite of her very poor health, however, and because she refused to perform compulsory labor, she was constantly tormented in the punishment cells of the prison. When they would take her away to prison for three or six months, she would leave me her lower bunk. Now she has returned to her family.

The other Orthodox prisoners were:

—Ekaterina Petrovna Alioshina, born in 1912, gentle and quiet, always smiling. She was very good at repairing footwear for all the female prisoners, she used to wait on the sick, and she prayed fervently. She has since returned to her people.

—Maria Pavlovka Semionova, born in 1923. She had been sentenced for the third time for the same "anti-Soviet" activity. In prison for over twenty years, she had been tormented for many years in punishment cells. Gentle and quiet, she used to care for the pigeons, feeding them under baked bread leftovers. She had artistic talent, and used to make beautiful collages. She prayed much. In 1982, together with Baba Yura Chvatkova, she was transported to exile in Kazakhstan.

—Nadezhda Mikhailovna Usoyeva, in her thirties, born in 1942. The youngest of the Orthodox women, she had been sentenced for the same reason as the others—the dissemination of

poems—to six years of camp and three years of exile. Like all
the Orthodox women in the concentration camp she refused as
a symbol of protest to perform compulsory labor, and for that,
she was tormented in the isolation cell and prison for a whole
six years. They would bring her to the concentration camp for
just a few days or weeks, and take her away again to torment
her with hunger and cold. I recall a description of Nadia I wrote
in a letter during this time:

> Nadia Usoyeva is a girl of remarkable goodness and
> tact (sentenced to six years of strict regime labor and two
> years of exile). She is a very decent and high-minded
> Russian Orthodox. We are like sisters, only unfortunately
> she was hardly ever permitted to 'take a vacation' at the
> labor camp. It's a real miracle; where does that fragile girl
> get her strength? Five years of punishment camp and strict
> regime prison with hardly a break—starvation, cold and
> ridicule. She is a true heroine before whom one should
> even kneel!
>
> Quiet, calm, always smiling, with a prayer on her lips.
> I never heard her utter an impatient or a rough word. She
> goes to the punishment cell smiling and returns smiling.
> Exhausted, blue with cold, she looks terrible, but smiles not
> only at us, but at her tormentors as well! Her example
> moved and still moves me to tears![17]

This last Nadia gives an opportunity to describe the prison
where those of us in camp were punished. She was completely
exhausted, her grey, blotched skin stretched over her skeleton,
but she was always calm and joyful, spending hours on end se-
cluded from others in the corner, in fervent prayer. And when,
after a few days of "rest", the warden would come again to an-
nounce with sadistic satisfaction that Nadia was being taken off
to the punishment cell that day, she would quietly get ready,
with a pleasant smile at the warden who would accompany her
out of our concentration camp to renewed torment. Only the

---

[17]From the *Chronicle*, No. 41, January 1, 1980.

good God could give a person superhuman strength and love for one's tormentors!

The punishment cell is a small, low cement cubicle in the basement, very damp and cold, almost unheated in winter, the temperature just a few degrees above zero Centigrade, with a little window near the ceiling.

Locking the prisoner up in the punishment cell, they take away all clothing, except for underwear; women are left with just a light striped summer-weight dress. Usually, they lock you up for fifteen days, without taking you out of the punishment cell once; there is an iron pot for nature's needs, a small stool and a little table cemented to the floor, and those are the "amenities".

To the damp, cold, concrete exterior wall which during the winter is covered with frost, is attached a bare board, half a span wide—the prison cot, which at 6:00 AM is secured with chains and locks to the wall, so that the prisoner will not be able to lie down during the day; and at 10:00 PM is unchained and lowered—for rest.

In order not to roll off that narrow plank, the prisoner is forced to keep his back pressed against the cold, damp wall. The starving, thinly clad prisoner usually cannot sleep for three or four days on account of the cold. After a while, he becomes semi-conscious.

Every other day, they give the prisoner a slice of bread, cold water and some salt; on alternate days, they offer a dipper of thin soup—*balanda*. And so, every other day, the prisoner receives a dipper of tepid liquid.

In the punishment cell, one is not given any reading or writing material. Besides the loneliness, cold and hunger, there are searches, vulgar ridicule and cruelty. Many criminals, unable to bear these torments, commit suicide.

This is how the sick, old Orthodox women were tormented for years on end simply because they refused to perform compulsory labor, until they were completely drained of strength, and admitted to the invalid section, where they did not have to work, but the torment of illness without remedies or serious medical care continued.

Prisoners in punishment cells are penalized for the slightest "infraction", e.g., for being too slow to stand and salute a passing guard. When they want to punish you, they can easily find a reason for it. They even lock up in the punishment cell sick women who are unable to perform their compulsory work norm on account of their weakness.

And what is the regular prison cell like? Here things are a little better than in the punishment cell, because at night they give you a little blanket for covering, and they do not strip you to your undergarments (but neither do they give you warm clothing). Daily, the prisoner receives a few spoonfuls of kasha, a cup of warm water and a dipper of soup—*balanda*. The food is worse even than in the concentration camp, and besides, one is locked up the whole time in the cell without air or sunlight—in a concrete coffin.

With the help of God, Nadia, like all of the Orthodox women, withstood those torments without her spirits being broken. After all these tortures, they took Nadia away for three years to Siberia. In Altay, she also suffered greatly, but now she has returned home. She returned with her health broken, but not her indomitable spirit. When I recall such spiritual giants as the pleasant little brunette, Nadia Usoyeva, I am reminded of the words from the gospel, "If God is for us, who can be against us?" It is possible for one who is deeply rooted in God and lives by love to bear all things. Love is unconquerable.

In 1975, the concentration camp also held six Ukrainian women. One of them, Nina Strokatova, was transported to the prison when I was brought to the concentration camp and from there they released her without bringing her back to camp, so that she could not meet the other prisoners and learn any news that she might carry out with her. Therefore, I never saw her. But she is now with her husband abroad, and can tell more than

I about herself and her fellow Ukrainian political prisoners.

Another of the Ukrainians, Nadia Alexeevna Svetlichnaya, born in 1936, served four years before returning home, and after much trouble also emigrated. Nadia is a good hearted woman who has suffered much, because when they arrested her she left behind her infant son, not quite a year old, whom the chekists did not turn over to Nadia's relatives for a long time, threatening to leave him permanently in the children's home. It is difficult to imagine what the mother's loving heart suffered! Nonetheless, in the concentration camp, Nadia was very polite, quiet and helpful and, like all Ukrainian women, she always used to join actively in hunger strikes and other protests on behalf of persecuted political prisoners. I am very grateful to her for her cordiality and for all her help while I was in the concentration camp. Afterwards, when I returned to freedom, she supported me morally from Siberia. May the Almighty God reward with His generous blessings her and all people who do good.

A third Ukrainian, Oksana Zenonovna Popovich, born in 1926, had been sentenced for the second time. The first time, she had not been quite twenty years old. Unable to stand the torments, she tried to escape, and was shot in the abdomen and hip. Miraculously, she survived. They sentenced her to ten years in the concentration camp, and exile for an undetermined period.

After all her sufferings, having gone through the hell of the Gulag, Oksana returned to the Ukraine physically an invalid, but spiritually unbroken. They put her in a hospital for an operation on her wounded leg, and from there, the chekists seized her directly to be tried again and sent away for seven years of concentration camp and five years of exile.

Her only "offense" was her love for the Ukraine and the truth, and her refusal to become a slave of the occupants. Oksana is very honest; she tells everyone the truth to their face, and this used to displease many. She could not stand any compromise with evil.

In the concentration camp she used to get around on crutches; her wounded leg which refused to heal was very painful; she suffered from high blood pressure (250/140 and higher); she was bothered by exhaustion and all sorts of ailments, but she was very sensitive to the sufferings of others. Presently, she is in exile in the Province of Tomko, where she was transported at the end of 1982.

Irina Mikhailovna Senik, born in 1926, was another Ukrainian woman serving her second term. The first time she was sentenced, like Oksana, when she was not quite twenty, to ten years of concentration camp and exile for an undetermined period. During interrogation, they tortured her, burning her, breaking her bones and beating her, even though young Irina was just a student, not guilty of anything. Her father had been a military officer, so the occupants, having tortured him to death, tormented his whole family. What Irina and thousands of the best people suffered has been described in the *Gulag Archipelago*.

After all her torments, she returned to the Ukraine. During a search, they found among her things a few poems written while she was still in the concentration camp, in which she described her own sufferings and those of others. For this they gave her an additional six years of concentration camp and five years of exile. She has just ended her exile, and returned to the Ukraine. Where she will be able to find a place is not clear. May the good God help her.

Her father was tortured and shot by the Soviets. Her mother was exiled, tormented in the concentration camp and died far from her homeland. Her thirteen-year-old brother Roman was tormented for not repudiating his father, and presently he is far from home.

These days, the chekists have begun to throw their weight around more than usual, and if Irina is not registered in the Ukraine, she may have to join her brother. Passport offices have received secret instructions not to register political prisoners who have been rehabilitated. In this way, an effort is being made to intimidate everyone, to subjugate even the most courageous to falsehood or to destroy physically those who remain loyal to the truth and sensitive to the sufferings of others.

"All of you should be shot!" the chekists tell the political prisoners to their faces, having given free reign to their hatred while their chief, Andropov, ruled the Soviet empire.

I met a fifth Ukrainian woman, Stefanya Mikhailovna Shabatura, during our transport to the concentration camp. Stefanya is an artist, born in 1938, who had completed higher studies. Completely grey and exhausted, she was tormented in a punishment cell and in the solitary confinement cell of the hard labor prison for almost a year, with brief breaks, just for demonstrating. She had refused to do hard labor because the administration of the concentration camp, at the instigation of the KGB, had confiscated and burned her pencil sketches drawn in her free time. Soviet officials fear not only words of truth and lines of poetry, but also innocent sketches—everywhere, they see danger for themselves, confiscate everything from the prisoners and burn it.

After her return to Lvov, they would not register her for her own cooperative apartment (obtained with her own money), in which her sick mother lived. After long trials, KGB intimidations and threats to jail her again (for not conforming to passport regulations: They refused to register her and for that, they threatened to punish her), Stefa was finally registered for one year, and she obtained employment.

The sixth Ukrainian woman, Irina Onufrievna Kalynec, born in 1940, used to write poetry. Intelligent and active in the concentration camp, after exile, which she spent together with her husband, poet Igor Kalynec, she returned to Lvov to her parents and daughter.

During my stay in the concentration camp, I found one fellow Lithuanian, Veronika Kodiene, born in 1916, a total in-

In this 1931 high school photo from a private collection are pic-
tured Canon Petras Rauda (second row, fourth from the left),
Nijole's mother, Veronika Rimkute (fifth row, second from the
right), and her uncle, Kazys Rimkus (fourth row, first on the
right), presently a physician in Chicago. Interestingly, Fr. Antanas Seskevicius is also in this class (second row from the top,
third from the left). It was Nijole's defense of Fr. Seskevicius
which led to her being placed under surveillance by the KGB.

Nijole Sadunaite at age 17 (left) with a friend in the capital city of Vilnius, Lithuania, taken in May 1955. She graduated from high school the following year.

At the wake of Jonas Sadunas (top), Nijole Sadunaite's father, who died on April 29, 1963, are (from right to left) Nijole, her mother Veronika, and her brother Jonas. All three are also present at his gravesite during his funeral on May 1, 1963.

Nijole Sadunaite at age 26 in 1964.

Nijole Sadunaite with Father Petras Rauda (middle), a Lithuanian high school chaplain who was a close friend of the Sadunaite family. The man to the left is unidentified.

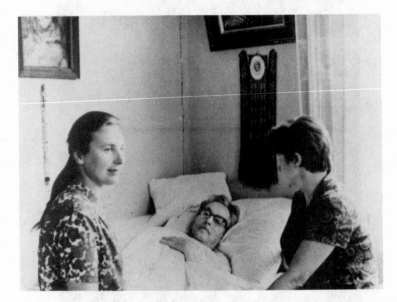

In this photo taken in 1973, Nijole Sadunaite is nursing Father Petras Rauda during his long illness. She took care of him until his death in 1974.

This is an excerpt from Nijole's manuscript, written in her own handwriting.

Home of Nijole Sadunaite in Vilnius (top); the "X" indicates the apartment from which she was arrested.

The desolate town of Boguchany, Siberia in 1977 (top), where Nijole Sadunaite spent three years in exile. Nijole is shown here in Boguchany during the same year.

Nijole Sadunaite in Boguchany, Siberia during her exile in 1977.

Nijole Sadunaite and friends in the Siberian town of Boguchany during her exile in October 1977.

Nijole Sadunaite in Boguchany, Siberia "sitting in the yard writing letters and enjoying the fresh air" during her exile in 1979.

Nijole Sadunaite in the Spring of 1981 after her return to Lithuania from exile in Siberia.

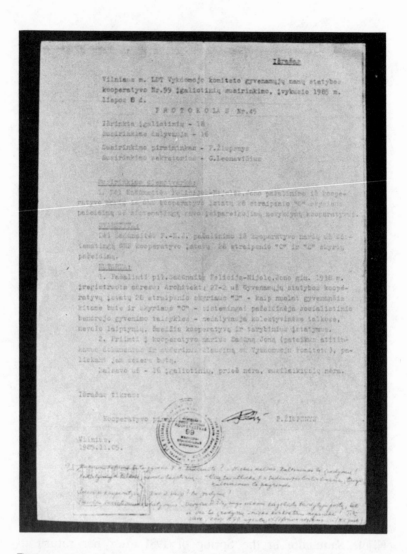

Document which summarized the meeting expelling Nijole from her cooperative apartment (refer to Part III in the text "No Home and No Work: The Harassment Continues").

The man Nijole refers to as Lithuania's "heroic martyr," Petras
Paulaitis (top), was well known as a member of the Lithuanian
Underground. He is shown here after his return to Lithuania in
October 1982 after 35 years of imprisonment in the Soviet Gu-
lag. He died on February 19, 1986. Nijole is shown with her best
friend Brone Kibickaite on her arrival to Boguchany in 1977.

Jonas Sadunas, Nijole Sadunaite's brother, is shown here with his wife Maryte Saduniene and his daughter Marija Sadunaite in a photo taken on May 7, 1983. Jonas was sentenced to one and a half years general regime labor camp at this time for fabricated charges of slander.

valid, whose nervous system was completely ruined. The KGB took her from the neurological section of the hospital, and sentenced her to ten years of concentration camp because, during the post-war years, in her home a *stribas* (a Soviet killer) was shot, and she did not report it, but buried him secretly. If she had reported it at the time, they would have burned not only her, but the whole village with all its buildings. The scourge of the Soviet killers is well known to everyone. Now she has returned to her relatives; I do not know what has happened to her since.

There was also a Russian woman, Galina Vladimirovna Silivonchik, born in 1937. She had married a Byelorussian and together with their brother, eleven years younger than she, had tried to leave the country. They shot her husband, beat her and her brother unmercifully, knocking out her teeth, and after that, kept her in the KGB prison and put her on trial.

Their father, who had abandoned them as infants along with their mother, had found himself another woman and refused to support them. Their mother, distressed, soon died. During the trial, he demanded the death penalty for his own children. He is a member of the "revered" Party. The court, however, sentenced Galina to thirteen years of concentration camp and five years of exile, and her brother, Yuri Vladimirovich, to eleven years of concentration camp and three years of exile. "Do not flee from the Soviet 'paradise'."

In the concentration camp, Galina was quiet, and would not join in protest and hunger strikes. When I arrived, she had already been in ten years. At present, she is in exile.

I also found in camp two KGB informers, the Ukrainian Jewess Natalia Francerna Gruenwald and the Jewess Anna Kogan. Gruenwald had worked for the Gestapo, had betrayed many people and killed them. For that, she received twenty-five years of concentration camp. But in the concentration camp she worked zealously for the Red gestapo, the KGB. She betrayed prisoners, libeled them, spied, and planted false information.

She did their dirty work, and for that, she received as recompense all sorts of privileges—supplementary parcels, patient's food, medical treatment, vitamins, etc.

Gruenwald was an elderly woman, over sixty years of age, with very malevolent eyes, which astonished me as soon as I saw her. Not without reason is it said that the eyes are the window of the soul. Accidentally, I myself heard how Gruenwald, toadying to the chekists, offered to testify that any of the political prisoners was emotionally unbalanced. . . . May God be merciful to her!

At present, after finishing her twenty-five year sentence, she lives in a home for the elderly, rejoicing that they feed her well.

Anna Kogan was transported to our camp from a criminal zone for purposes of spying. She and Gruenwald used to keep an eye on us: who was friendly with whom, what we talked about, who organized strikes and the writing of protests and petitions. She also interfered with our attempts to establish contact with other concentration camps—she used to hang on the chekist's apron strings.

When they used to demand that we tell them how we found out what was going on in other concentration camps, we would reply, "We have found this underground telephone . . ." Before I even came to the concentration camp, a young Russian mother of two, Raya Ivanova, had been sentenced together with some Orthodox women. When the chekists could not rehabilitate her, two of them, with the help of Gruenwald and Kogan, drafted a statement declaring that Raya was emotionally disturbed. They shut the completely healthy, calm and good-hearted Raya Ivanova up in a psychiatric hospital in Kazan, where after a year, unable to stand the torments, she died. May she rest in the Lord! She is one more martyr for the Faith and for the love of God.

The concentration camp physician had said, "If Ivanova is a mental case, then we are all three times crazier than she is." But, the KGB later hounded that doctor from his position. Meanwhile, the poor KGB informers, Gruenwald and Kogan, took advantage of all kinds of privileges in the concentration camp. They used to have milk every day and ate white bread and butter (patient's diet), which the sick never saw. For her "good" work, Kogan was released a half year early, after 6.5 years. In this way, the chekists buy themselves lackeys, and being killers, make use of the services of former killers, and are inseparable friends with them.

Camp Politics

Right near us, a few hundred meters away, was the male political prisoners' fifth zone. We used to correspond secretly with that concentration camp. As soon as they brought me to the camp in 1975, we found out that a chekist agent had seriously beaten the Ukrainian poet Vasily Semionovich Stusa, born in 1938, in revenge for the fact that they could not break his spirit. They threw him, battered and bloody, into a punishment cell, claiming that he was to blame for a fight. A torturer received a supplementary package.

Learning of this, all of the Ukrainian women and I proclaimed a hunger strike, demanding that the prosecutor come and sentence the real culprit, and put Stusa in the hospital. In our petition, we wrote that we would fast until our just demand was honored. They isolated all of us, shutting us up in a ward of the psychiatric hospital. After five days of our fast, the prosecutor came and put Stusa in the hospital for treatment. He had an operation for an abdominal hernia, after which they granted him a certification as an invalid of the second class, unable to do any hard physical labor.

Soon afterward, they transported Stusa to exile. In the course of the transport, they revoked his invalid's certification, as though he had become well, and, transporting him to Magadan, compelled him to work in the mines. Immediately after he had returned from all those torments, Stusa was tried again. Several KGB agents were summoned to Magadan, and testified during the trial that, in Magadan, Stusa had spoken out in an anti-Soviet manner.

They sentenced the ill, completely exhausted and tortured poet (during interrogations they tortured him physically) to ten years of strict concentration camp and five years of exile, without giving him an opportunity in court for a final statement.

In addition, he was sued for 1000 rubles, for the travel expenses of false witnesses. Andropov's chekist pupils are walking in their former chief's footsteps. . . .

My own case, however, was not so hard. The chekists were seriously concerned lest the details of my trial get out (recall that they did not permit any witnesses to remain in the courtroom after testifying and, as soon as the trial was over, they transported me under special guard to the concentration camp). In Lithuania, the KGB embargoed the mail of everyone suspected of having a connection with the *Chronicle of the Catholic Church in Lithuania*. They did everything that they could to see that my trial remained a secret. The chekists seek to escape world scrutiny; they fear the light, and they will do anything to have people live deceived by lies or paralyzed by fear.

But God was good. I was able to write a description of my trial and send it out. The letter reached its final destination by hand, avoiding the snares of the KGB. A twentieth century David overcame Goliath, since he fought in the name of the Lord. For that, to the good God alone, be glory and thanks!

To the chekists, however, it came as a great surprise. The Moscow KGB disciplined them for stupidity. The poor chekists in Vilnius, with Lieutenant Colonel Markevicius at their head, came to Mordovia in the summer of 1975, not long after I had been brought to the concentration camp, and summoned me to the warden's office. There were Markevicius, some other chekists and the editor of some paper waiting for me. At least that was how they introduced themselves. Chekist Markevicius said, "We have come to take you home. We will set aside the penalty on one small condition. Don't tell us whom or how, just tell us where you were able to smuggle out the news about your trial, and you'll go home free."

I answered them, "I travelled a whole month to reach this paradise of yours, and I don't want to leave it without finishing my sentence. As for the thing you're interested in, I won't talk." And so, they left Mordovia without getting anything from me, while I learned from them that the good God had blessed my efforts.

All the more active political prisoners, after they finish their concentration camp sentence, are taken away for so-called "rehabilitation". They are usually taken for two months to where they were sentenced, in the hope that their resistance may have been worn down, and they will be susceptible to attractive promises. The basic means used by the chekists to deceive people are lies coated by hypocritical cordiality; and when the deception does not work—threats and fear. Soviet policy is based on lies and deceit, violence and terror.

In the concentration camp, I used to join actively in all demonstrations, often acting as liaison with political prisoners of the other concentration camp, so that life in the zone never lacked drama. It has been rightly said: "When the stomach is empty, the head is clearer." Prisoners' minds are indeed clear and inventive. The poor chekists, in spite of all their efforts, never did discover how we found out so quickly what was going on in other concentration camps.

As revenge, even though they never caught me, at the end of my term they revoked my right to receive a five kilogram package. In three years of concentration camp, I received only one five kilogram parcel. Prisoners in the strict regime camps are not allowed to receive anything for half their term, and after that, if they do not break the rules and the camp administration permits it, they may receive one five kilogram parcel a

year—in which there must not be anything high in calories except for baked goods, butter, meat and fish! From active prisoners, even those parcels are confiscated on the basis of fabricated
allegations of violating the rules. It is only the grace of God
which sustains those under sentence; this is why they are all
very grateful to those who remember them in prayer.[18]

In April, 1977, they took Galina Silivonchik and me from
the concentration camp, without telling us where or why. They
treat all prisoners this way: the warden comes in and tells you to

---

[18]Despite repeated efforts, no letters from relatives and friends in
either the United States or England ever reached Nijole. British newspapers wrote that over 200 letters sent to Nijole from England were
returned. Even from Lithuania, not all letters reached the labor camp.
One particular example of this is on October 31, 1975, Fr. Seskevicius
wrote Nijole a registered letter, return receipt requested. Only when
he asked the Gargzdai Post Office to inquire why the labor camp had
not notified him whether the letter had been given to Sadunaite, did
the labor camp post office give notice by telegram that his letter had
been received on November 5th, not by Nijole Sadunaite, but by
Camp Censor Devayev. Moreover, censors removed from the letters
religious pictures, Christmas and Easter greetings, even the prettier
postcards. Also, not all of Nijole's letters reached their addresses.
During January and February, 1977, KGB censors intercepted two of
Nijole's letters.
Between March 13, 1977, and May 13, 1977, Nijole was held at the
Saransk interrogation facilities in Mordovian ASSR. She contracted
bronchitis. She often ran a high temperature. She returned from
Saransk with a more serious case of bronchitis, and again with a high
temperature and complete physical exhaustion. Because she did not
receive proper medical attention, this developed into bronchodilation.
In the meantime, the camp food and other conditions completely undermined Nijole's strength. Her health grew worse.
At the end of the winter, Nijole wrote: "I am fortunate at work
since I always fill the glove-sewing quota. Now things will be somewhat harder, for I am weak. But that's a trifle, spring is nearly here.
The grasses will awaken, and with them, I will find renewed strength,
for we eagerly eat dandelions, pigweed, and flower blossoms. They
contain vitamins and calories." (Information taken from the *Chronicles*
of October 1, 1976 and June 29, 1977.)

prepare in fifteen minutes or less for transport. Slaves are not told why or where they're being taken. Thus they drove Galina and me like cats in a bag after returning to us all our property from the storage room, as though we were never coming back to the concentration camp.

When our "raven" stopped, it was already dark. They herded us to the third floor of a large brick building, and locked us up in a small cell. Some time later, they told us to report to the doctor. I began to think that they had brought us to the psychiatric hospital in which the chekists were constantly threatening to confine us, but it became apparent that the two of us had wound up in Saransk, the KGB interrogation isolation prison for "rehabilitation".

The medical aide asked what our complaint was and took our temperature. The soldiers searched all of our "property" and afterwards, locked us both up in larger cell. The rehabilitation began. Some soldiers escorted us to see the prosecutor. In the office were sitting two chekists. One of them told me, "We'll allow you to go home, and you won't have to go into exile, if you promise, on your return to Lithuania, not to tell what you experienced during interrogations and in the concentration camp—if you keep quiet when you get home."

I replied that I had remained silent until my arrest, because I had nothing to tell about, but now I would speak because there was something to say. They warned me that they would make my exile one hundred times more difficult then conditions in the concentration camp. To this, I replied, "The harder, the better!"

The chekists glanced at one another and, surprised, said, "What character! We like you!" and they never mentioned the subject again during interrogation.

They decided to try another tack. They summoned the teacher of Marxism-Leninism from the school for higher studies to disprove my views. The chekists left us two women alone in the office, to give the impression of a cordial conversation. Just about my age, she was very surprised to see me, since she did not expect that I would be so joyful and cordial to her. We began talking. I soon became convinced that she did not have the slightest notion about religion, and I said to her, "Please forgive my frankness, but back home in Lithuania, six and seven-year old children know more about religion than you, who teach your students atheism. How can you deny and resist something you do not know?"

She readily agreed that she had no knowledge and had not even read the Gospel. She became interested when I told her about the power of prayer, and God's mercy to people. Afterwards, she said, reflectively, "I can't believe that people would be punished for practicing their religion."

"It's too bad," I replied, "that you are unable to get acquainted with my case file, which is in the offices of the Vilnius KGB. There, for ten months while they were interrogating me, the chekists examined all three issues of the *Chronicle* found in my possession during the search, issues giving examples of those who had suffered from practicing their religion; they did not find a single thing to be untrue. You can't get hold of the *Chronicle* to get acquainted with it, but that's not necessary; you can prove it for yourself."

"How?" she asked, surprised.

"It's quite simple," I explained, "just go to the Orthodox Church in Saransk to pray, as though you were a believer, and you'll see that soon you'll drop your job like a hot potato!"

After a moment's thought, she replied that it would really be so. We did not pursue the subject, for at this point some chekists who had probably been eavesdropping on our conversation came in and told us to stop talking. The instructor asked that she be allowed to talk with me again the next day. The chekists sternly replied, "You are not allowed. It's not you who are educating her, but she you!" I never saw her again; I just remember her and her little daughter in my prayers, since she did manage to tell me something about herself.

At the Saransk KGB, another surprise awaited me. Galina and I were put up in a good, well-lit cell, not in the basement, but on the third floor, where we could see the tops of the trees through the window. In order to make sleeping more comfortable on the wide wooden benches used as beds, they brought us each two brand new straw mattresses; they offered us each a third mattress, but we declined.

Besides all these privileges, they fed us very well. Although one is allowed to purchase only five rubles of food products per month in the concentration camp, the Saransk KGB allowed us to purchase 30 rubles worth, or more—of course, from the money we had earned ourselves. The soldiers would bring from the shops fresh milk, cream, cheese, butter—whatever they could get, we never dreamt of such delicacies. The two of us were fed almost as well as a president.

Galina and I joked, "Easter is near, the Soviets have no meat, so they are fattening US up for the slaughter. . . ." They used to take us out in the prison yard for exercise when we requested, when the sun was shining, and not just for a half-hour, but for three hours. Only the isolation prison warden asked us not to tell anyone. We did not promise. After my conversation with the instructor on atheism, I was almost never summoned for interrogation, or rehabilitation. While in the concentration camp, I had become ill: I was weakened by a serious cough.

For a couple of months, I was treated in the concentration camp hospital, where the food is very poor, but you don't have to work. In Saransk, they began to give me formal medical treatment. They took me to the polyclinic for a checkup. After that, the medical aide used to dispense foreign medication every day, and at bed time she used to apply hot suction cups and mustard plasters. We did not have to work; during the day we used to read books obtained in the KGB library.

The cell window had one row of bars, and we could open it whenever we wished. The weather was good. In this way two months passed and I regained my strength, developed a suntan and became unlike a prisoner. Then one day, the warden of the isolation prison summoned me and a soldier escorted me. The warden said to me, "We would like to photograph you, because your brother is very concerned about your health."

I refused, saying, "My brother just visited me in the concentration camp. Very soon, they will transport me into exile where he will be able to visit me again. I refuse to be photographed."

I suggested that they photograph Galina, who had not seen her brother for eleven years. The warden muttered something to himself, as if to say that was not necessary, and asked again that I agree to be photographed. I refused categorically.

The soldier took me back to my cell, but less than a half-hour had passed when I was summoned by the prosecutor. They brought me to him. At the Saransk KGB, we did not wear the striped prisoners' uniform, but our own clothing which they returned to us from the storeroom when they transported us from the concentration camp. The soldier ushered me into the interrogation office,

I was surprised to see a large decorated room, with soft chairs and large unbarred windows. Behind a round, lacquered table sat two chekists, while a third stood on one side; all of them were smiling pleasantly. My "re-educator" said, "How good you look! One would think you had just returned from Paris."

"And how does Saransk differ from Paris?" I asked him. He invited me to sit next to him on the sofa. I declined. Then they drew an ornate armchair up to the table, and I sat down. One of the chekists began to tell me, "I come home, and hear that my neighbor is back. I go over to see him, and I am surprised that he has his door locked. Why? 'Ah ha, I say, 'He must have gotten his hands on a piece of meat somewhere, and is in a hurry to eat it himself, so he won't have to share it with me'."

I smiled at the fact that the chekists also talk about the shortage of food products in the Soviet Union. At that instant, a light flashed; the young chekist standing by had photographed me. Only then did I understand why the whole comedy had been put on.

"Why, you're abusing your position," I said to him. "You've photographed me without my consent. God grant that my picture not come out!"

The photographer, quite satisfied with the shot, replied, "I've been working here as a photographer for four years already, and there has never been a time when one of my shots has not come out." With this, he left the room.

My "re-educator" explained to the visiting chekist, "They've made a goddess of her abroad, yelling and screaming that she's dying. Let them see how good she looks!"

For two months, the chekists kept me as though at a resort, just to disinform those abroad: "See what our Soviet prisoners are like!" The following morning, the warden of the isolation prison summoned me again, disturbed, he said, "Your picture didn't come out yesterday." He showed me a very sharp post-card-size photograph of me sitting in the armchair, smiling but with bars in front of me. I'm literally sitting behind bars and smiling. There were bars across the entire photograph.

The warden told me that the bars appeared because the photographer did not use the right film. He asked me to agree to be photographed again, but I refused. A soldier escorted me to my cell, and after a few minutes, took me to the prosecutor's office. Instead of being met by the prosecutor, I was met by the photographer from the day before who took me into his dark-room. I sat down on a simple chair at a table, and he begged me very emotionally to agree to be photographed; otherwise he would be in trouble.

I began to feel sorry for that poor chekist, took a magazine from the table, placed it on my lap, and bending over it as though reading, I said, "Now you may photograph me." He made his preparations, and requested, "Raise your head and smile." To this I replied, "Photograph me reading, or else I will not cooperate." He took the picture, "Only please never ask God again not to have my pictures come out! I believe in God, too, only I don't have the strength, will-power or courage to admit it."

The photographer himself confirmed that it had been impossible to develop my photograph in the normal fashion, not on account of the film, but because of the power of prayer. How good God is! He tries to bring the wanderers back to Himself.

Some time later, I was summoned by chekist Tresoumov, who had arrived from the concentration camp in Mordovia. He had been drinking considerably, and boasted that he had been celebrating his fortieth birthday. He invited me to be photographed with him, or to accompany him to Vilnius to see the sights, and other nonsense. I absolutely refused. Then, in hopeless anger, he said, "Who needs your sacrifice. Take everything you can get from life here and now, because tomorrow you will croak and no one will remember you."

I told him that people don't "croak", they die. He angrily rebutted me and continued, "You or I may already be suffering from cancer; we'll croak, they'll plant us, and everyone will forget, even our friends and relatives."

How much terrible despair in the heart of a chekist who is only forty years old!

After two months, Galina and I were taken via the exhausting transport back to the concentration camp. On the way, I came down with a cold and the cough and fever—my chronic bronchitis—began to torment me again.

Back at the concentration camp I found out that the male political prisoners had refused for three months to carry out compulsory labor, demanding that in the Soviet Union political prisoners be classified as such. The women in our concentration camp were exhausted; no one had enough energy left to take on three months of new torments in the punishment cell.

My sentence was the shortest, my exile in Siberia was just around the corner, so fresh from Saransk, I wrote the concentration camp superintendent a petition demanding that we be acknowledged as political prisoners, and protesting against new political arrests in Lithuania (I had found out that they had arrested Vladas Lapienis), I refused to do any compulsory labor till the end of my concentration camp term, August 27, 1977.

The concentration camp administration immediately summoned me to convince me to retract my statement, saying that it would be pointless, and for me it would simply mean new torments in the punishment cell. They reminded me of my poor health, and the fact that I faced the difficult journey to Siberia.

"All of your petitions and protests are just a drop in the ocean, and you will gain nothing, but just ruin your health," said the superintendent.

"So let it be a drop to help someone else," I replied, "after all, drop after drop can wear a hole in a rock. To make things easier for others, I'm ready for anything, not just the punishment cell, but even death."

The recurrence of my acute bronchitis and a temperature of 100° F kept me out of the punishment cell, although the chekists forbade me to be treated. Besides, male political prisoners told the administration that if I were sent to the punishment cell with a fever, they would proclaim a hunger strike. Throughout that whole time, they never gave me a single letter, and they used to confiscate my letters to my brother.

Exile

Toward the end of my term, they took me away to exile without, of course, telling me where. My journey to Siberia lasted a whole month, with stopovers at transfer points in Potma, Chelyabinsk, Novosibirsk and Krasnoyarsk.[19]

---

[19]Nijole described in one of her letters in more detail the terrible ordeal she endured on her way into exile: "I left Barashev on August 24th. The camp's head bookkeeper came to see me just before I left and told me to write her a letter when I reached my destination, giving my address, because otherwise she would not know where to send my money. . . . And if it weren't for good people, I would have to starve until my first salary. That would certainly not be healthy after a difficult twenty-day journey. Thank God there are good people everywhere and they helped and continue to help me in many ways.

"I spent one week each in the Chelyabinsk, Novosibirsk and Krasnoyarsk prisons. There is no need even to speak of cleanliness and other hygiene necessities. By a lucky coincidence, I managed to avoid getting lice. I fought the bedbugs with all my might, and the women who have become accustomed to them laugh heartily at my expense. To my misfortune, I did not learn to sleep with the bedbugs biting. . . .

"During the trip I had the flu and an ear infection. There was no medical attention, and now, as a souvenir, I have one deaf ear. . . . Thank the Good God that the other hears well. It would be wonderful if I completely stopped hearing curses and obscene language, but could only enjoy the kind words and the polyphony of nature. (From the *Chronicle*, No. 30, November 1, 1977)

On the way to Novosibirsk, on September 5, 1977, in a packed railroad car, I suffered a heart attack. The female criminals in my compartment, noticing that I was deathly pale, began shouting that I was dying. I, too, felt that I was at death's door. I had no sensation in my hands or feet, which felt like they belonged to someone else, completely numb; my vision faded and I could no longer hear anything. However, in my heart was a deep peace, even joy: "Thank God it's all over!" I thought. I was just sorry for my brother, who would be tormented by not knowing how or where I took leave of this life.

But it was not God's will yet to have me depart this world. The soldiers quickly brought medicine and water, and opened a window. When I recovered somewhat, I asked them where they would have put my body if I had died. They answered that they would have left it in the prison at Novosibirsk.

They transported me together with female criminals; and I was with them in the same prison cells except in Pskov, where they kept me isolated. I had nothing with me in the way of food or clothing; anything decent I had left at the concentration camp, since the need was greater there, so there was nothing to take from me. It sometimes happened that the female criminals, seeing that I had nothing, used to share their food with me. They were very interested in my case, and the fact that I was being transported into exile. There is no exile for female criminals, and they thought that it was only in Czarist times that people were hauled off into exile.

"You're going to be in exile just like Lenin," they said. Being together in the same prison cell for a week at a time, we used to talk a lot. I never disguised my beliefs; I used to say grace before and after eating, pray, tell them to their face that their lives were wrong, and that living as they did, they would never be happy. I used to be very kind to them because they were so unfortunate.

Feeling, perhaps, that I sincerely wished all of them what was good, they were all good to me in return, and I never experienced from them any injustice or derision. Altogether, I was with the female criminals four months: two months in transport and two months in the hospital.

In the Novosibirsk Prison, I spent a week with three women from Petropavlovsk, sentenced to fifteen years for murder. When they were just barely thirteen, they had begun to engage in robbery, together with a fourteen-year-old boy. In the evening on out-of-the way streets, they would assault lonely passersby, maiming or even killing them, and then taking their money. They took nothing but money, of which they never found much. "After all, we have to live," they said. "We need something for booze, for butts and to get decked out." They had begun smoking at the age of ten.

They complained that they had been too severely sentenced, since "they hadn't done anything." One of them had been given two years, another two and a half years, and a third, as ringleader, was given, I believe, three years or a little more. As minors, they would not have to serve half their sentence. Female criminals are always being amnestied. The terrible thing was that they did not consider their barbarous behavior a crime, but a normal phenomenon: "We have to live."

These are the fruits of atheism. "If there is no God, anything goes!" Who can count those millions of dehumanized prisoners who, behind barbed wire, live a truly hellish life, brimming with the worst kind of amorality, cruelty and hatred. Although it is truly said that the Soviet Union is one great concentration camp, only the degrees of discipline differ. People from whose hearts God has been torn sink relentlessly into a morass of rottenness, considering evil to be good, and being ashamed of the good. Only when I ran into those unfortunates did I appreciate what a great treasure is faith in God, and how great is our resulting responsibility. Are we doing everything possible to help others?

At the end of the transport, I found myself at the prison at Krasnoyarsk, where I spent a whole week in a cell, half underground, packed with female criminals. The transfer points—huge prisons—are everywhere overcrowded. This is the one area in which the Soviets annually exceed the plan, and the numbers of unfortunates are constantly growing.

From Krasnoyarsk, in order that my exile truly be a hundred times worse than concentration camp, as the chekists in Saransk had promised, they decided, on orders from the KGB, to take me out to the taiga, together with eight male alcoholic criminals, to cut timber. In the taiga, the bear is the prosecutor, the wolf is the attorney and criminals ride roughshod. This is how the chekists planned to carry out their words uttered in Vilnius: "Say goodbye to Lithuania, you'll never see her again! You're in our hands, and we're going to do what we want with you!"

But the poor things did not know that we are all in the hands of God, and that without His consent, not a hair falls from our head. How different are the thoughts of short-sighted human beings from the plans of God!

From the prison in Krasnoyarsk, they flew me and the eight criminals to Boguchany, four hundred kilometers north of Krasnoyarsk. In Boguchany, they took us in a van to militia headquarters, from where they were supposed to drive us sixty kilometers out into the taiga. However, that day, September 19, 1977, the van which was supposed to take us broke down, and we stayed overnight in Boguchany. Even in the militia yard in Boguchany, three of the criminals were arguing over whose "prize" I would be. I trusted in the protection of our Heavenly Father, and remained calm.

The militia building stood on the bank of the Angara River. I admired the beautiful Angara, about two kilometers wide at Boguchany, winding nobly among the forest-covered hills. The leaves, with their autumn coloring of yellow, green and red, reminded me of the Lithuanian tri-color. It was a sunny day. I thanked God for nature's great beauty and for His love for us, who are so unworthy of it.

After a while, I was summoned and told that at the request of the criminals, the cleaning lady for the detoxification center had agreed to take me home for the night, so that I would not have to spend the night on the floor in the high-ceilinged cell of the center, with the eight alcoholics in whose company I had been brought there.

Our warden agreed to let me spend the night at the lady's house, ordering her to bring me back at nine o'clock in the morning to the militia station, from where they where supposed to take us to the taiga. He did not let me go to the post office, which was nearby. I wanted to send a telegram to my brother in Vilnius, and let him know where I was, since he had not received a single letter from me in four months.

"When you get to where you're going, you can write then," a militia official told me. The cleaning lady took me home. Her little house was just across the street from the militia buildings. She told me that they were taking us to the taiga, where there were no inhabitants for a radius of forty to fifty kilometers, and no transportation, except for occasionally passing vehicles. Anyone coming to visit me would have to go on foot, and look for me out on the taiga, and of course, it would be impossible to find me.

I inquired whether they needed a cleaning lady or dishwasher in Boguchany, since if I could remain there, it would be easier for friends and relatives to visit me. I discovered that there was a two-story school where seven cleaning women were supposed to be employed, since the school had two shifts. Only two were working, and a third had been discharged for excessive drinking.

While we were speaking, the school's charwoman, Anya, my age, approached. We arranged with her to call on the manager at eight o'clock the next morning, to see whether she would employ me as a charwoman. "If they don't take you," said Anya, "I'm going to quit on the spot. I'm working for three-and-a-half people and they're paying me for only two-and-a-half. I'm exhausted!"

They were glad to hire me, since no one else was available; everyone drinks too much. The militia officer in charge of exiles agreed to leave me to work and live in Boguchany; for this the poor man got into trouble with the KGB. How dare he leave me in Boguchany without their knowledge! By September 20, 1977, I was working as charwoman in the Boguchany Middle School, and living with Anya in the apartment assigned to her by the school.[20]

Only that evening were the eight criminals transported out into the taiga. Obtaining some cheap moonshine somewhere, they became intoxicated and got into a fight. They killed one of their number, and dismembered the corpse; two of them they maimed, breaking their hips and splitting one's head. I later saw one of them in the hospital in Boguchany, recuperating, and the others I met by accident in the street. They all assured me that I was very fortunate, because if I had gone with them to the taiga, I surely would not have lived more than a day.

"We drank ourselves into a white-hot fever, and we can't remember what we did. The militia didn't show up until four days after the fight, when the injured began looking for help and the corpse was already putrid," they told me.[21] Thus, the

---

[20]Nijole's reflections in a letter at this time reveal her extraordinary character: "And so, I am free again! What a great joy that is! I fill my lungs with the pure taiga air. I rejoice in the space, in the innocent eyes of children. Thank the good Lord for the beauty of nature, for the spark of kindness in the souls of people!" (From the *Chronicle*, No. 30, November 1, 1977)

[21]Nijole's reflections in a letter while she's in exile are pertinent here: ". . . Without the grace of God, man is the most miserable of beggars. That is loudly evidenced by the millions of spiritual paupers who have not had the fortune to know and to love the Good Lord, and have been wandering the backroads of life since childhood. I met many of them on my journey. And regardless of how low they have fallen, the spark of goodness which a kind word ignites smoulders in each of them. How very essential is God's grace to their souls, so long tortured by evil! Let us pray, let us sacrifice, because the ranks of

KGB's plan to destroy me physically failed.

At the middle school, the work was hard. Outside it was muddy and after recess, the pupils returning to class from the school yard, would bring in so much dirt that it was necessary to slave from morning until late at night.[22] The dormitory cook, seeing how hard I worked, took pity on me and told me that the hospital needed a nurse's aide, and that job would be easier for me.

In October, 1977, I was visited by Brone Kibickaite and Liudas Simutis, the latter having served twenty-three years in a concentration camp. What a pleasure the visit was! The three of us, after cleaning the schoolrooms and corridors, went for a walk and together thanked the Lord for everything.

Brone Kibickaite and I went to the hospital, where they agreed to hire me for the maternity ward, since I was a certified

---

spiritual paupers are growing by leaps and bounds. I saw for a fact how miserable man is without God. (From the *Chronicle*, No. 30, November 1, 1977)

[22]As Nijole wrote concerning her job in Boguchany: "The middle school has not yet been repaired, and our students are studying in the grade school, in a second shift, from 2:00 PM. We also go to work in the afternoon. We ring the bell for classes and recesses, we keep the hallways clean, and after classes, we give the building a thorough cleaning. There was a huge amount of work to do because there were too few cleaners, and Anya and I had to do the work of four. The day before yesterday, a third cleaner was hired and now it's much easier. Besides, my strength is slowly returning. This shows how important freedom is! Ten days in freedom and I am already standing more firmly on my feet, and even a strong wind no longer frightens me. My weakness is passing, I tire less at work and feel that I will soon be as strong as before—in freedom.

"My money from the labor camp has not yet been sent. If it were not for good people, I would have had to starve.

"I get along with the people, everyone is friendly and good to me. I also try not to be indebted to anyone. We live very harmoniously.

"My sincerest to all who remember me!

"May the Good Lord bless and keep all of you!" (From the *Chronicle*, No. 30, November 1, 1977)

nurse, and had worked in the children's home. They promised me a private room in the dormitory.

On November 1, 1977, I began working in the Boguchany Hospital. The hospital's chief of staff, a former exile and Lithuanian, Mecislovas Butkus, was on vacation when I went to work. He was not even in Boguchany at the time. Nevertheless, they later constantly harassed him for employing me, and the KGB demanded that I be discharged. However, the courageous doctor would reply, "She's doing good work, give me a written order to discharge her, and I'll do so."

The KGB never beats you with its own hands, but uses the hands of hirelings and intimidated people. When they could not intimidate the chief of staff, they began to circulate malicious rumors. Militiamen went about Boguchany telling the residents that they had brought a believer to town, who had gone to work in the hospital, and was now poisoning mothers giving birth and their newborn, giving them tablets poisoned with "little angels". Moreover, she was supposed to have in her possession a radio receiver and transmitter, sending all sorts of state secrets abroad.

Thus I was painted as a terrible criminal, and no one was supposed to have anything to do with me, speak with me or even sell me anything. Otherwise, they too would become state criminals. For some time, people feared and avoided me, but this lasted only for a few months.

The first to find me in the hospital were the Baptists. We became good friends and used to pray together. In Boguchany there were about fifty of them, many of them young and active. I'm very grateful to them for their moral support and friendship. They accepted me like a sister. May the good God reward them!

They joked about the fact that if it weren't for the stories originated by the KGB, they would never have come to know me. But when the militia began to repeat the nonsense, they became interested and found me. Thus, for those who love God, all things work for the good.

When the KGB became convinced that it was too good for me in Boguchany, they ordered me through the chief of militia to decertify myself, to quit my job and to move north to the Village of Irba, as a milkmaid. It was December of 1977, and the temperature was reaching -40 to -50° C. As I wrote in one of my letters at this time:

> ... My "good" times in Boguchany are coming to an end! One and a half months at the school, one and a half months at the hospital—exactly three months since I've come to Boguchany, and now the good news: I am leaving it for the Village of Irba.... (December 20, 1977)
> The Village of Irba is 100 kilometers [62 miles] from Boguchany. When the weather is good, an airplane arrives at 12:20 PM our time on Tuesdays, Thursdays and Saturdays. Cows are milked by hand, work begins at 4:00 AM and ends at 10:00 PM without any days off. The people drink, no one works.... (December 23, 1977)[23]

Ilya Glazer, who was then a political prisoner in Boguchany, and is presently in Israel, advised me somehow to delay leaving until January, 1978, because on January 3 he would end his exile and, returning to Moscow, would organize support for me so that I should not be forced to go off to a second exile on the Irba Soviet Communal Farm.

I thanked him for his concern, and said that things would be the way God wanted them—for me, His will was more important than anything else. I quit my job and reported to the Chairman of all the Soviet Communal Farms in the area, so that he might arrange for my employment as milkmaid at the Irba Communal Farm. The Chairman, surprised, asked why they were assigning me to such a hard labor: The communal farm was backward, there was no feed, the milkmaids were drunkards and I would have to work every day without a break, from early morning until night, doing my own job and that of others.

---

[23]From the *Chronicle*, No. 31, February 2, 1978.

I told him that they had promised me the most difficult kind of exile, that I was not afraid of work, but that I would not be much of a milkmaid since I suffered constantly from fever, and would not work for long. The Chairman was glad to hear this and, wishing to help me, said that he did not need any sick milkmaids. He referred me instead to the hospital for a checkup. Accepting his recommendation to the hospital, I returned to militia headquarters to tell them that I was being instructed to get a physical examination.

The militia chief was not in, and I saw his assistant. Entering the office, I heard the assistant speaking with a young, dark-haired man about me. When I approached them, the assistant said, "Here is the new milkmaid I told you about. She is educated, industrious and most importantly she doesn't drink at all."

I asked the assistant why he was sending me to a second exile, if according to him, I was so well recommended. "Is the KGB giving you a difficult time on account of me?"

He turned to me and, covering his mouth with his hand, told me quietly so that the Irba District Chairman, sitting in his office would not hear, "If you understand, then why do you ask?"

I then told him that I was not being accepted as a milkmaid, but being sent to get a medical checkup. The assistant replied that even if I were unable to do work, I would still have to leave Boguchany. They did not need a milkmaid as much as they needed to make life as difficult as possible for me. The militia was carrying out this KGB instruction.

They put me in the therapy section for a medical checkup. The head nurse of the section herself checked my temperature every three hours, distrusting and burning with hatred toward this "fascist". She, a member of the "revered" Party, believed all the KGB's stories. At night, my temperature would be normal, in the morning up a little, and by evening, up to 100 or 101 degrees.

I was bothered greatly by a cough, but they would not give

me any medicine and the woman doctor in the therapy section who was supposed to be treating me feared me like the plague, and did not approach me in the ward once. It was no joke; I, a "public enemy and a fascist', could bring the wrath of the KGB down on her. It was better to keep away from such a woman.

The head nurse catheterized my stomach, and afterwards, my bladder. The test continued about six hours, until blood appeared. I was rescued from that torture by a laboratory technician who came into the ward. Frightened, she withdrew the catheter and said that one must not remain with a catheter inserted more than three hours. This catheterization was the reason why, a month later, I came down with Botkin's Syndrome (jaundice). As for my temperature, the head nurse said, "Think of it, 101 degrees! Is that a fever? That's just the right temperature for a milkmaid to work!"

I remember as though it were yesterday the terrible tragedy of Christmas Eve, 1977. A young nurse's aide came into our ward and in a voice trembling with emotion, told a patient who was an acquaintance of hers that in the gynecological section, they had discarded a newborn girl in a unheated storeroom, and for two days she had been crying, and would not die.

Taking some clean water, I asked the nurse's aide to show me there. On a little table painted white, wrapped in a thin receiving blanket, lay a tiny girl, her face already blue with cold. When I touched her, she began crying weakly. I baptized her, and hurrying out to the nurse's office, I found them chatting lightheartedly. It was already late at night. Upset, I asked them why they had thrown the innocent child out to die of starvation. Angrily, they retorted, "It's none of your business. The doctor knows best who should live and who die."

I replied that it was a doctor's duty to save life, not to destroy it. By killing their own infants, they were acting worse than the fascists who killed only foreigners. They began shouting, "Get out of here! You must have escaped from the nuthouse to feel sorry for everybody. It's our business—we do what we want!"

Leaving with a heavy heart, I went to the doctor on duty, but she was of no help, either. Right here was a maternity hospital, special cribs for premature infants, warmth and food. But for this child, there was no room there. Never in my life have I had such a sad Christmas. The little girl lived until morning, and when they reported it to the obstetrician who came to the gynecology section, she said, "She should have been thrown out into the scrubbing bucket long ago!"

Such is their "crystal pure" Communist morality! They have no sympathy for their own innocent infants. So what hatred must they feel for those who think differently.

In the hospital, I also met a woman patient who worked at the Irba Soviet Farm taking care of calves. She described the chaotic conditions at the communal farm. There was no feed, everything was neglected and cows and calves were dropping like flies. They wanted to deduct the cost of the dead calves from their pay even though they were not exiles.[24]

"But we're not to blame that there is no feed," she exclaimed, "I came to Irba with my husband because they promised me an apartment, and now I really regret it." It was December, and there would be no salary until May. Most of them were drunk and there was no one to do the work. There were fights and murders. She warned me that I must not under any circumstances go to Irba. They would sue me for neglecting the cows and for those which had died, I would have to pay the

---

[24]Nijole wrote in a letter around this time about the evils of Irba in more detail: ". . . I have been told clearly by people living here that there is no state farm more backward and neglected than Irba. . . . Against me they would probably fabricate a case for the deliberate destruction of animals, with a serious indictment. This thought was voiced by the Siberians themselves. Wages are not paid, some have not been paid since May; there was no bookkeeper, there is complete chaos. Mud, rats, chaos. People are fleeing Irba. As local residents say: 'A brothel is no place to live'." (January 6, 1978) (From the *Chronicle*, No. 31)

state compensation which I would not finish until I died. I thanked her for her kindness, but it was not for me to decide whether I went to Irba or not.

When they discharged me from the hospital, January 10, 1978, certified as healthy and able to do any kind of work, regardless of my night fevers of 100 degrees, I went back to the militia. The chekists had come from Krasnoyarsk to see the militia chief, and I was told to wait outside his office. After sitting around for a good hour, I decided to go in and ask when he would be free to receive me.

When I entered his office, the militia chief was talking with two chekists. Seeing me, he stood, and spreading his arms, said with a smile, "So you're staying here to live and work?" I did not understand why everything had changed so suddenly, and I replied that it was not my idea, but it was he who was telling me to leave. The chief of militia interrupted me, saying, "Live and work in Boguchany!" Once again, the good God had arranged it so that I remained in Boguchany until the end of my exile. The love of God is especially felt at life's difficult moments. Glory, love and thanks be to Him forever!

In Boguchany, I used to receive many letters and packages from abroad.[25] The postmaster wondered and asked me what

---

[25]Nijole wrote more about her correspondence in a letter about this time: "I had begun to worry when for a long time I received no letters from my family living in Vilnius. But today I am celebrating! The mail came, and among other letters there were five letters from my brother Jonas Sadunas. Apparently a letter finds it sad 'to travel' by itself, so it waits for companions: It's more fun when there are five!

"Many of my notes of only a few sentences do not reach many labor camp inmates, prisoners, exiles, inhabitants of Moscow. . . . Many of my letters disappear during the long journey to my homeland, Lithuania. . . .

"The customs duties imposed on gifts received from abroad are very high. Chocolate is the most expensive food item: 1.20 rubles per bar. A package of cocoa is 3 rubles. Fees for claiming clothing are very high. (It doesn't matter whether the clothes are new or used.) An ordinary, synthetic sweater is 25 rubles, a chiffon scarf 20 rubles,

people from twenty foreign countries were writing to me. "They write that they love me and are praying for me," I would answer. I would repack the parcels I received and send them to political exiles whose conditions were more difficult than mine. I knew about twenty of them. Again, the postmaster wondered why I sent everything not home to Lithuania but to utter foreigners out in the backwaters of Siberia, Yakutia and Magadan. He asked who those people were to me.

"They are my brothers and sisters in trouble," I would answer. "Even you say that man is brother to man." Girls in the Communist Youth Organization would wonder and ask, "If we fell on hard times like they, would you send us parcels too?"

"Of course, if I had your address." To them, it was incomprehensible, but they took my word for it. After I had returned to Lithuania, I received cordial greetings from them, saying that they could not forget me. Real love is more powerful than hatred!

---

stockings 5 rubles. Prices are the same as in the stores or even higher. And my basic pay is 75 rubles per month. I pay 20 rubles for a small six square meter room. . . ." (From the *Chronicle*, No. 39, July 22, 1979)

Freedom and Persecution

On July 7, 1980, my exile ended and I flew home by way of Riga, Latvia. Alighting at the Riga Airport, I was met by a white Volga from the Vilnius KGB; without any documents or order, they seated me in their car and took me to Vilnius. It appears that Father Alfonsas Svarinskas and a few other priests and faithful had come to Riga to meet me. They wanted to take me to the festival of the Blessed Mother at Zemaiciu Kalvarija.

Chekists from Riga chased them out of the airport. The chekists spirited me away so there would be no welcome. In spite of all the KGB threats, very formal welcoming ceremonies were arranged for me in many parishes in Lithuania in which a large number of children, youth and adults participated. I would tell them of my odyssey: my arrest, interrogation, prisons where I was incarcerated, the concentration camp and Siberia, always emphasizing that throughout those six years, I often felt that without the will of God, not a hair falls from our head.

We must all trust in Him and not fear any persecution, but work as much as we are able for the good and the glory of God. Fear is the beginning of betrayal. We have to fear only that we work and worry too little about the things of Christ and the Church, and there is too little sacrifice in our lives. Let us not be chary of ourselves. Let us lean on Christ and we shall be unbeatable.

Meanwhile, even after my exile, the KGB would confiscate most of my letters, and through the prosecutor's office, they would threaten to imprison me together with female criminals. They began to carry out their promises when the former KGB Chief Andropov, became ruler of the Soviets. The chekists gave themselves free reign and began throwing their weight around as never before.[26]

After returning from Siberia, I wanted to get work as a cleaning woman in a store, but the order was given in the cadre section that such work was too good for me, and if the directess took me on, she would be driven from her job. Afterwards, I obtained employment at the church in Pabirze, as a helper, doing laundry, taking care of church vestments, the sanctuary and the gardens. For that, like all church employees, I pay the state

---

[26]From the *Chronicle*, No. 45, Oct. 22, 1980: "Following the trial of Dr. Algirdas Statkevicius, between September 11-16, the prosecutor's office of the SSR officially warned Nijole Sadunaite, Andrius Tuckus, Algiridas Masilionis, Genute Sakaliene and Vytautas Bogusis that they behaved improperly at the trial, and they were warned not to attend any more trials.

"Nijole Sadunaite is free, but her persecution continues. While in exile, she was deprived of many letters from abroad, but most of them did eventually reach her. After returning to freedom, she wrote letters to her friends abroad, but did not receive a single reply in four months: Soviet censors confiscate them all. Gifts to Nijole are also confiscated. . . ."

From the *Chronicle*, No. 48, June 29, 1981: "On June 11, 1981, Nijole Sadunaite wrote a statement to the Chief Judge of the Lithuanian SSR Supreme Court, requesting a copy of the verdict in her June 16-17, 1975 trial, because the document of the court verdict had been confiscated from her by the Barashev, Mordovia, labor camp administration the day she arrived at the camp and had not been returned, despite her written requests that the document be returned. On June 24, Assistant Judge M. Ignotas of the Lithuanian SSR Supreme Court sent the following reply to Sadunaite's request: 'This is to inform you that a copy of the verdict in your criminal case was given to you once, and copies of verdicts in this type of case are not issued a second time'."

income tax. But this restriction of employment was nothing compared to what followed.

First, as revenge against me, they decided, as they had promised earlier, to take care of my brother. They trumped up charges against him and shut him up in a psychiatric hospital. The very day after they confined my brother, on November 19, 1982, I sent an urgent telegram to my uncle in the West, saying, "They have put Alius in a psychiatric hospital. Nile." At baptism, my brother was given two names, Jonas Aloyzas. My uncle in his letters calls him Alius and me Nile. My uncle, as far as I know, did not receive that telegram; no return receipt reached me, although I paid 21 rubles and 64 kopeks to send the telegram, almost an entire month's salary.

The KGB from Vilnius seized the telegram which had been sent to my uncle, and in response to my letter, November 22, 1982, a provocation took place. I went to the psychiatric hospital to visit my brother. I was set upon by the head of the section, KGB agent Dr. R. Razinskiene and expelled: "Get out of here! You have no right to visit this place!" No sooner had I left than she made a phone call and a chekist visited me incognito, the one who had been in charge of the raid on our place in October, 1982.

He and his militiamen had hoped to catch me before I could get off the grounds and regretted missing me. Under the direction of a chekist, they put together a report saying that I had insulted Dr. Razinskiene. No matter how she treated her staff, the untruthful report was signed only by two Poles, Nurse Jadwiga Staszinska and medical aide Czeslaw Czernewski. All the other workers and persons present refused to sign, and many of them suffered for it, especially those who had managed to speak with me.

The KGB is especially annoyed by the fact that their criminal activities are transmitted abroad as soon as they happen. Then the poor things complain that they are being libeled, and they confine innocent people to prisons and psychiatric hospitals. According to a bit of folk wisdom: "The more they beat you, the more they yell!"

That same day, they brought David Seveliov who had come from England at his brother's invitation, from the psychiatric section to Section 1, which is under the jurisdiction of the KGB. His brother works for the KGB: they wanted to recruit David but failed, and shut him up in the psychiatric hospital.

In Section 1, a person is "treated" in such a way that after two months he does not know his own name. They do not allow anyone to visit Seveliov, nor is he allowed to receive food parcels. Others, who were with him, including a twenty-year-old German man from Maisiogala, were shut up for their religious beliefs. At Mrs. Razinskiene's orders they used to receive massive daily injections of aminazine, and spent the whole day in a kind of sleep. Sometime later, they took the young German away and shut him up in the psychiatric hospital of Cherniakovsk. In this way Mrs. Razinskiene, with the help of the KGB, takes care of recalitrants. May God forgive her!

The next day, three militiamen with a van and documents came to take me, but that time, with the help of God, I was able to slip away. Many times afterwards, the KGB and the militia have looked for me on various pretexts. I have been avoiding those "comrades", only because I would still like to be of as much service as the Lord allows to people struggling for the truth and for their rights. I am ready at all times to go to prison joyfully, and if the Lord should grant such a grace—to die for that.

On June 8, 1983, the Supreme Court in Vilnius, in response to my brother's appeal, commuted his sentence on May 24, 1983, to eighteen months of conditional compulsory labor. On July 6, he was put to work on the Soviet farm in Giedraiciai as a brigade member in the plant conservatory section. The position had long been unfilled because no one wished to work with chemical herbicides harmful to one's health. On July 24, I spoke with my brother by telephone, and he told me all about it. Immediately afterwards on July 26, on the basis of hastily telegraphed orders from the Ministry of Internal Affairs, he was transferred to a construction job in the City of Jonava. The Superintendent of Construction was surprised that although there was nothing against him, he had been transferred from Giedraiciai where as an agronomy specialist he had been very necessary, to do very hard physical labor, digging and mixing concrete, when there was no shortage of labor here.

Not quite three months had passed when my brother had a hernia operation. He suffers from chronic pleuresy, angina and bronchitis. Several years ago, the doctors forbade him to work in the field as an agronomist, on account of his poor health. This was why he had transferred to the experimental institute. Now he was working with criminals on construction, living in the dormitory to which he must return immediately after work. He is allowed to visit his wife and seven-year-old daughter Marija in Vilnius only on days off. Each time, he must register with the militia.

On September 15, 1983, they placed my brother in the Jonava Rayon Hospital, Tuberculosis Section, because they found a spot on his lungs. He suffered night fevers of 101 degrees and complete hoarseness, complicated by acute bronchitis. The next day, he received a summons from the KGB to report September 19 to chekist Vidas Baumila in Vilnius, for interrogation.

Frightened, my brother's physician, Doctor Matulioniene of the Tuberculosis Section, gave him verbal permission to go for the interrogation, even though the journey from Jonava to Vilnius and back took about six hours.

On September 19, chekist Baumila interrogated my brother for three hours. He showed my brother letters from me, Vladas Lapienis and Petras Paulaitis written from camp, copied over in my brother's hand, which Jonas had kept stored in his basement archives, so they wouldn't be destroyed. However, the basement was torn up and the copies of the letters seized. The chekist accused by brother of handing those copies over to Father Sigitas

Tamkevicius, saying that they had found them at the priest's home during a raid.

My brother said that he did not know who had torn up his basement and taken the copies of the letters, nor did he know where they had put them. He had never given anything to Father Sigitas Tamkevicius, and if the chekist claimed that he had found them in the possession of Father Tamkevicius, let him produce a record of that search. The chekist would not show a search report, but began shouting and threatening that they would bring a new case against my brother.

He inquired about me. My brother replied that I was working and lived in his apartment, with his wife. In spite of threats, my brother would not sign the report, saying, "You have already forged my signature under statements drawn up by yourselves, and later put me on trial for it."

Chekist Baumila ordered my brother to come to the KGB the next day for interrogation, since it was the end of the working day. On September 20, Baumila interrogated my brother again for two hours and fifty minutes. He repeated the threat that he would be tried for giving information to the *Chronicle of of the Catholic Church in Lithuania*. Here he lied, saying that Father Sigitas Tamkevicius had admitted that my brother had given him the copies of those letters.

My brother requested a confrontation with the priest. The chekist, alarmed, began again to shout and changed the subject. He began threatening my brother that they would not forgive him for betraying a "state secret", because my brother had written a petition to the chief of the KGB in Lithuania, in which he revealed that the chekists had tried to recruit him as an informer.

My brother repeated to the chekist, as he had said in his petition, that he was would remain faithful to his Christian conscience. Then the chekist took my file and began trying to convince my brother what a terrible criminal I was. He said that I was passing information abroad and that the next day they were going to arrest me. They threatened to sentence me to many long years of imprisonment. They were very annoyed over the fact that my brother's petition to the chief of the KGB immediately got out abroad. They demanded to know to whom my brother had given the petition.

Once again, my brother refuse to sign the report, attesting that the KGB was forging his signature. Moreover, he stated that they did not need to interrogate him any longer concerning Father Sigitas Tamkevicius, nor to subpoena him, because he would never give the chekists they testimony they needed. Baumila threatened to keep my brother until he signed. When my brother refused to be intimidated they released him, with the additional threat that they would avenge themselves for everything.

At 3:00 PM on July 22, 1983, in a black KGB Volga, the chekists picked up my brother's wife, Maryte Saduniene, from her place of employment. She works as an occulist at the Vilnius Polyclinic. They took her to KGB headquarters and began demanding that she turn over underground literature which, according to the chekists, she had received two weeks previously.

Maryte replied that she had not received anything, and that if the chekists knew so much, then they should have picked up that literature themselves. The chekists would not give their names, saying, "The day is past when we gave names." They tried to force Maryte to testify that if I did not stay home—that I was a vagrant. Maryte told them that I was living and spending nights in my apartment, but that I often returned late when she was already in bed, and left early, before she arose. And so often it happened.

Maryte signed the record of her interrogation, since they threatened not to release her until she signed, and she had to pick up her little daughter, who had been left at the Polyclinic. Now she is seriously worried lest the chekists falsify her testimony.

Releasing her, they threatened to bring her to trial, just

like her husband, and not just leave her in peace.

On June 13, 1983, I sent Andropov and the Chief Prosecutor of the USSR many petitions signed by believers in Lithuania protesting the unjust sentencing of Father Alfonsas Svarinskas and the criminal arrest of Father Sigitas Tamkevicius and his incarceration in the KGB cellars under the libelous accusation of anti-Soviet activity. These petitions were signed by tens of thousands of believers in Lithuania. All of these petitions I sent in my own name and with my own return address. The KGB, unable to avenge themselves on me directly, began terrorizing my brother's wife. May the Lord be merciful to them all!

Part III: AFTER HER RELEASE

Under God's Protection

As I mentioned, in the forenoon of November 23, 1982, I visited my brother Jonas Sadunas, who was confined in the psychiatric hospital of Nauja Vilnia for observation by the KGB. The KGB was tormenting my brother just because they had failed to enslave him morally and because of their desire to detect and destroy the editorship of the *Chronicle of the Catholic Church in Lithuania*. Back in 1974, the KGB investigators who had arrested me boasted that in a month or two there would be no more *Chronicle of the Catholic Church in Lithuania* because all had been discovered. Twelve years have passed, and the *Chronicle*, with the help of God, still survives. For that, praise and thank the Almighty!

In any case, the medical chief of the psychiatric examination section, KGB agent Razinskiene, ordered me out and with a chekist who came to her assistance, fabricated a trumped-up charge against me for allegedly insulting her. Expelled by Dr.

Razinskiene, I left immediately. I quickly crossed the broad hospital courtyard. Approaching the side gate, I saw pass by several militia cars, one of which stopped not far from the gate, behind the bushes, as though to be concealed. Standing right at the gate was a taxi, with its door open. I was very fortunate, since taxis never stood there. Apparently, it had brought someone and had not had time to drive away. The driver agreed to take me to Vilnius, and at my request, he let me off at the Gates of Dawn. The Solemnities of the Mother of Mercy had just ended. I wanted to thank the Blessed Mother for her protection, and to commend my brother's needs to Her.

After thanking the Mother of Mercy of the Gates of Dawn, I spoke by phone with my brother's wife, Maryte. Describing briefly the events at the hospital, told her I would not be home, and asked her to take the men confined with my brother some bread, which they lacked. I then went to the home of an acquaintance, and drafted protests to the Minister of the Department of Health and to the Attorney General of the Lithuanian Soviet Socialist Republic. I immediately mailed the protests, and the texts appeared in the *Chronicle of the Catholic Church in Lithuania*.

Late that night, I went home to prepare for a raid. I learned that Dr. Razinskiene had that very day informed my brother that a criminal case had been brought against me, and she regretted that I managed to get away. Right after I had left, the militia and a KGB agent arrived. My brother immediately drafted protest letters describing the fabrication. That day, many militiamen waited in the hospital courtyard for me to visit my brother again, but they were disappointed.

Early on the morning of November 24, the anniversary of the murder of Father Bronius Laurinavicius, I left home disguised as an elderly lady, just in case some KGB agent was waiting in the yard. On the sidewalk in front of our door, a man was pacing back and forth, obviously waiting for someone. Bent under the "burden of age", and limping somewhat, I immediately turned to the other houses on the left instead of to the street to the right, which was the usual route downtown.

Lazdynai is a new suburb of Vilnius. I went unhurriedly. Behind some bushes, I noticed that the man, actually stooping, was following me with his gaze. He must not have recognized me, because he remained at his post.

Leaving the courtyard a few houses behind me, I stepped up my pace and not meeting anyone, I crossed Lazdynai. I took the trolley-bus downtown, and stopped into the church of the Holy Spirit (formerly the Dominican Church) to pray. During the Holy Sacrifice of the Mass, I resigned myself completely to the will of God, repeating the words of the little Saint Theresa of Lisieux, "I desire nothing but what you, Oh God, wish and as you wish it! . . . Lead me where you will, the way you know, for you are truly Love!"

My heart was at peace. After praying, I went to the home of my best friend, Brone Kibickaite, whom I often visited, and keys to whose apartment I had. The KGB knew this and when they summoned me to warn me, they used to mail the summons to both addresses, mine and Brone's.

My friend had already gone out. Unlocking the door, I entered that apartment and soon lay down to rest; the night before, I had almost no sleep, preparing for the raid. I immediately fell fast asleep, and slept for several hours. Suddenly in a dream, I saw two militiamen in uniform, and understood that they were looking for me. Immediately I heard the doorbell, a long, insistent ring.

If it had not been for that dream, I would have opened the door. Now however, I crept to the door and, climbing up on something, I looked very carefully through the transom. Outside the door, I saw the caps of two militiamen. Quietly I climbed down and went back into the room, determined not to open the door. Through a back window overlooking the yard (the apartment was on the second floor), I saw a white *Nova* militia car parked at the entrance to the building, with a uniformed militiaman seated at the wheel. The KGB had decided to take care of me through the hands of the militia.

"Well," I thought, "let's see what happens." My heart was beating wildly and the doorbell kept ringing insistently. Finally, it stopped. Soon, I saw the two militiamen come down the stairs into the yard. One of them carried under his arm a brown folder which was most likely the order for my arrest.

After a brief conversation with the driver, they all drove away. I immediately left Brone's apartment. And so, thank God, this is the fifth year that the entire force of the KGB, with all their agents and assistance of the militia, has been looking for me in vain, pursuing me fruitlessly. How real the words of Psalm 117 (118) have become for me, "With Yahweh on my side, I fear nothing: what can man do to me?"

Some say that I am very shrewd. This is not so! To attain His ends, God often chooses the most unlikely people, and that's what I am. "What appears to the world to be weak, God has chosen in order to confound those who are strong," writes St. Paul. One thing I know, that those who trust in the Lord will never be disappointed, and every day after Holy Communion, I speak to Jesus paraphrasing St. Paul, "Who shall separate me from your love? No, Lord, even the fear of death shall not separate me from you, for you are my life; neither the love of this life for I am prepared to sacrifice it for you; nor the powers of heaven for you are more powerful than they; nor the things of the present, for they pass; nor those of the future, for I love none of them more than you; nor suffering, for you comfort me; nor oppression, for you fortify my heart; nor hunger, for you satisfy me; nor poverty, for you enrich me; nor danger for you comfort me; *nor persecution, for you defend me*; nor the sword, nor suffering, for they would be sweet to me for love of you; nor slavery, for in you, I would find freedom; nor finally freedom itself, for I wish to be the slave of your love; nor the creatures of this world, for they are nothing compared to you; nor the transiency of the world, nor the wiles of my foes, nor my own weakness, for you will turn all those misfortunes into good for me—nothing shall separate me from the love of Jesus Christ!"

And I ask the Blessed Mother to allow me to love the Good Lord in Her Immaculate Heart. This is the extent of my "shrewdness".

After November 23, 1982, I would visit my apartment in Lazdynai, and Brone, only stealthily. And the good Lord protected me from the eyes of the people of ill will.

No Home and No Work: The Harassment Continues

Why did they take away my cooperative apartment on July 8, 1985? I quote the minutes (no. 45) of the representatives' meeting of the Vilnius Residential Housing Construction Cooperative No. 99, held July 8, 1985:

> Representatives elected: 18
> Participating in the meeting: 16
> Presiding over the meeting, P. Ziupsnys
> Secretary of the meeting—G. Leonavicius

Agenda:

Whether to expel Felicita-Nijole Sadunaite, daughter of Jonas, from membership in the cooperative, for infraction of Section C, Par. 28 of the Regulations of the Cooperative, by systematically failing to fulfill her obligations to the cooperative.

Discussion centered around the expulsion of Felicita-Nijole Sadunaite from the cooperative for systematic infraction of Articles C and E of the Regulations of the Cooperative.

It was decided:

1. To expel citizen Felicita-Nijole Sadunaite, daughter of Jonas, born 1938, registered at Architektu 27-2, for infraction of Art. 28E of the Regulations for the Cooperative by living regularly in another apartment, and of Art. C—by systematically breaking the rules of socialist communal living by not participating in cooperative social projects, does not clean the stairs, libels the cooperative and Soviet law.

2. To accept as a member of the Cooperative Jonas Sadunas (contingent on submission of the appropriate documents and after consultation with the Executive Committee), assigning him to his sister's apartment.

Voting for—16 representatives. No opposing votes and no abstentions. Signed: P. Ziupsnys—Chairman of the Cooperative

Of course, no one has proven that I have another apartment, since no one knows where I live. I'm a free woman and come home whenever I please. My brother's wife, Maryte, participates in the Cooperative projects and keeps the stairs clean. Where and how I have libeled the Cooperative? These are vague, meaningless words. Likewise, with regard to Soviet law, there is no proof, but this the KGB should be concerned with, and not Ziupsnys. Here the poor man only gave himself away as a KGB agent. KGB Investigator Gudas threatened to take away my apartment back in 1970, and in 1974-75, KGB Major Vytautas Pilelis did so. What is an apartment worth compared to eternity? How joyously I repeated with Saint Francis: "God is mine and everything is mine."

I am the happiest woman in the world because God loves me, watches over and protects me. Strange as it may seem, in December, 1986, they called my brother from the Executive Committee and told him that I had not been expelled from the cooperative and not been stricken from the registry. Only the good Lord knows what that means, and that suffices. God has his plans and they govern. There are human plans, and they do not govern.

Another example of this truth can be found in the state's effort to deny me work. When I returned from exile in Siberia, the KGB would not allow me to take a job, not even as charwoman in a store, so I obtained employment as assistant to the charwoman at the church of Paberze. The Providence of God makes all things work out for the best. In this job the KGB was unable to keep me under surveillance; I used to work when there was work to be had. Many times, I tended the fire beds, planted flowers, watered them, weeded them and, in the fall, I would gather up and burn the leaves fallen in the churchyard.

I used to help the old sacristan to keep the church in order. I never hid away from the people who came to help out, or to see the pastor on business. After work, I used to take part in evening devotions, and afterwards I used to go to the sacristy to write down that I had done this or that chore. I paid income tax. Many warned me that I was not circumspect enough, since the KGB was looking for me so tirelessly.

The Vice Commissioner of the Council for Religious Affairs, Jozenas, came to visit me when I arrived at the home of Father Donatas Valiukonis, pastor of Paberze. He asked whether I really worked there, and bemoaned the fact that I did not live in my own apartment. The pastor vouched that I was employed, and Jozenas left, having accomplished nothing. Going against Goliath in the Lord's name, little David will always be the winner! Trusting in God, let us do everything we must; without His permission, even a hair from our head shall not fall. God is our refuge and our strength!

My years as a fugitive are witness to that. The KGB is looking for me not only in Lithuania, but in Latvia, the Ukraine, the heart of Russia and even Moscow. They have interrogated and investigated all of my acquaintances who ever wrote me letters during my exile in Siberia.

The whole time I have been living in Vilnius, frequently and even daily visiting the families of prisoners of conscience under surveillance by the KGB, going to visit one or the other church in Vilnius, helping to prepare my brother's little daughter Marija for First Communion, and riding to work. So I wasn't exactly acting like a fugitive. God used to help me avoid encounters with KGB agents. Sometimes I would spot them before they saw me, and sometimes others would warn me, and I would disappear in time. There were many incidents in those years. One cannot write write about them all. Only one thing is clear: God does not abandon those trusting in Him. For everything, praise and thanks to the Almighty!

Unable to settle matters with me, the "comrades" began to terrorize my brother's family. Here are a few fragments: After 8:00 PM on October 10, 1985, my apartment doorbell rang. The stairwell was dark. To my inquiry, "Who is there?", someone answered, "Militia! Please put on the stairway light!"

The electric switch was next to the doorbell, so that one could see who was standing at the door. They did not put on the light; the doorbell just kept on buzzing, accompanied by cries of "Militia! Militia! Militia!"

One of the neighbors went out on the landing and turned on the light. Now one could really see that a uniformed militiaman was standing at the door. They opened the door. An official in the uniform of a militia lieutenant entered my apartment, and without even greeting or showing his official credentials, began shouting angrily in Russian, "Why wouldn't you let me in? What are you afraid of? Perhaps you have a lot of gold?"

"We were afraid of robbers. We have been burglarized twice already. If we don't see who is ringing the doorbell, we won't let you in next time, either! Besides, even now, we don't know who you are, since we are seeing you for the first time."

"I am an inspector from the militia," the visitor introduced himself.

"Not long ago, we were visited by another inspector from the militia, who left us his visiting card with his name and telephone number," my relatives answered.

"On account of people like Sadunaite, militia inspectors have to be changed frequently." And suddenly he asked, "Is Nijole Sadunaite here? When will she be here? Where does she work? Let her present her work permit. I'll come back in a week, and if Nijole Sadunaite's work permit is not here, then I'll be coming back to see you every day."

Then he demanded that they produce their papers, and taking out some sort of writing, he told them, "I don't have the right to show you this document," and he placed it on the table.

While he checked their papers, my relatives had read that the documents had been written on October 3, 1985, addressed to the Chief of the Department of Internal Affairs of the Spalio *Rayon*, Militia Lieutenant Colonel S.H. Blazhv. The document states: "The officers of residence Cooperative No. 99 inform you ... that Nijole Sadunaite has not been living in her cooperative apartment for five whole years, is not working anywhere. . . . She was sentenced to six years for anti-Soviet activity. . . ."

The document was typed, a whole page. It was signed by Chairman Petras Ziupsnys of Cooperative No. 99. Poor Ziupsnys should be treated for hardening of the arteries, for in the fall of 1982 he and two "comrades" checked everybody's passports in our building himself. Taking my passport, he ridiculed my incorrectly entered name (the passport had been issued after my exile, and they copied my name incorrectly).

He also made fun of a little picture of Christ which I had placed in the cover of the passport. All that I recall well, but he, the poor man, "forgot". After checking the passports and telling me that everything was in order, he left. So it was three years and not five since Ziupsnys had seen me. He wrote that I was unemployed when he had my certificate of employment. Such is the Soviet "truth". May God forgive him the lie, since this is the atmosphere in which he was reared.

After checking their passports, the militia inspector inquired why I had not obtained employment in Vilnius. They explained to him that since I returned from exile in Siberia, I was refused employment, even as a cleaning woman in a store. And so, I had obtained work as an extra worker at the church in Paberze, and that I earned about 27 rubles a month, after taxes. On the spot they produced my income tax receipts for several years. They explained that my certificate of employment had been submitted to Ziupsnys on June 24, 1985, during a representatives' meeting of the Cooperative, and that Ziupsnys himself had read the text of that certificate of employment to everyone out loud. All thirteen representatives at the meeting heard it.

"I need a new certificate of employment for Nijole Sadunaite," the militiaman insisted.

"Our former inspector had Nijole Sadunaite's certificate of employment, and it should be in your files," they explained to the inspector.

"But I need a new certificate of employment for Nijole Sadunaite," my visitor insisted.

To the question how many times a year new certificates of employment can be obtained, there was no reply. After a brief silence, the inspector asked under what paragraph I had been sentenced.

"We don't know, because the Mordovia camp administration never returned Nijole's copy of the decision to her, even though she requested it several times in writing. When after her return to Vilnius from exile she wrote a petition on June 11, 1981, to the Chief Judge of the Supreme Court of the LSSR, requesting a copy of the decision. Associate Judge M. Ignotas of the Supreme Court of the LSSR responded to her petition, saying that *in cases of this nature*, copies of the decision are not issued a second time."

Finally, the inspector, after saying that they would be meeting more than once, left without saying goodbye. The conversation had lasted about an hour. After he left, my brother's nine-year-old daughter, Marija, ran up to him, saying "Daddy, that militiaman yelling outside the door, 'Militia! Militia! Militia!'

scared me so much!"

Marija threw her arms around me and asked, "What would they do to you if they caught you? I love you very much and pray for you every evening!"

"Be calm Marija! The prayer of innocent children is powerful, and so only the best will happen to me," I replied. The fear disappeared from her wide, dark eyes, and she smiled.

The poor inspector terrorized and threatened my brother and his wife several more times, but he also decided to frighten Marija. On November 1, 1985, my brother was admitted to the hospital. The diagnosis was tuberculosis of kidneys and eyes. In November of that year, when my brother's wife was working until 9:00 PM, and her daughter Marija was home alone, the militiaman would come and bang loudly on the door, shouting to her to let him in. After the first scare, the girl's mother came home from work to find that her daughter had locked herself in the bathroom, terrified. Marija had told her that the militiamen had come, shouting loudly and banging on the door, so she had hidden in in the bathroom so that if they put the light on in her room, they would not see her.

Another time, her mother found her sitting under a desk. Next to her stood a table lamp, and Marija was doing her homework. Although her eyes were full of terror, she smiled at her mother and said, "Mommy, I have become tougher! I'm not afraid of that militiaman. Let him bang on our door and shout outside!"

The third time, there was a woman with Marija, who helped to remodel the apartment. When the militiaman began banging on the door and shouting, the woman opened the door and let him in. The militiaman assailed the woman, "Don't you know that anti-Soviet people live here? Why are you painting the walls of their apartment?"

The woman calmly replied that to her, all apartment walls are the same. After that, the militiaman inquired where my brother was, saying that he had to go for interrogation.

My brother was transferred from the Vilnius City II Hospital on November 27, 1985 to the clinic of the Tuberculosis Research Institute, where he was treated until January 8, 1986. From January 9, 1986, he lay in the Republic Tuberculosis Sanitarium of Kulautuva, from which he was discharged on June 20, 1986. The definitive diagnosis was tuberculosis of the kidneys and left eye. This was a result of constant colds while he was undergoing compulsory labor in construction. Let all those sufferings be dedicated to the greater glory of God and good of souls!

For their part, my brother and his wife have commended themselves completely to the will of God. Although my brother is presently employed at the Vilnius Inter-*Rayon* Plant Quarantine Station as a technician with a monthly salary of 105 rubles, he must still endure harassment on my account. Chairman Ziupsnys of Cooperative No. 99 would not desist, assiduously carrying out orders from his KGB "comrades". For example, on September 29, 1986, during a meeting of representatives, Ziupsnys attacked my brother for not bringing me.

"Nijole is not a child, so that I should have to bring her. Besides, you evicted her from the Cooperative fourteen months ago."

Ziupsnys then said, "Nijole Sadunaite must reclaim from the state bank any payments she has made for her cooperative apartment."

My brother requested that Articles 30 and 75 of the February 28, 1983 Decree of the LSSR Council of Ministers be read. Ziupsnys read Article 30: "The balance of the assessment is to be returned to a member resigning from the Cooperative when the new member accepted by the Cooperative pays his assessment." They then handed my brother a statement saying that 6,148 rubles and 86 kopeks had been deposited in the state bank.

Ziupsnys said, "We will give her a month's time. If during that time Nijole Sadunaite does not reclaim from the state bank the sum she has paid in, her money shall be transferred to an escrow account. If, within three years she does not reclaim her money, the deposit of 5,040.50 rubles will revert to the state."

Moreover, he angrily demanded, "Where are you hiding Nijole Sadunaite? Where is she living? I haven't seen her for five years! The residents of the Cooperative haven't either!"

My brother asked, "If no one has seen Nijole for five years, then why did you state at the board meeting of July 8, 1985 that she was libeling the Cooperative and Soviet law? Who heard Nijole libeling the Cooperative?"

"Nijole Sadunaite transmitted libelous material over Vatican Radio," Ziupsnys insisted.

"Did you hear that material?"

To my brother's question, Ziupsnys replied, "Everyone heard how that Vatican Radio libeled our Cooperative."

"And where's the proof that Nijole gave them that information?"

To this question, the secretary of the meeting, G. Leonavicius replied, "If we have libeled Nijole Sadunaite, then sue!"

"You have expelled Nijole from membership in the Cooperative unjustly, because she has no other apartment," my brother explained. "Can you produce the address where Nijole is living permanently? Without her address, you were not supposed to expel her from the Cooperative."

To this, Ziupsnys replied, "Nijole is travelling all over the Soviet Union. That's why she is not living with you."

"But there's no stated time limit for a member of the Cooperative not to inhabit an apartment!" my brother retorted.

Ziupsnys was silent. It would be interesting to know whether it was from the KGB that Ziupsnys learned that I was travelling all over the Soviet Union, since he stated that for five years, neither he nor any other members of the Cooperative had seen me. Witnesses like poor Ziupsnys testifying in Soviet courts against prisoners of conscience say what the KGB wants them to say. Such is everyday Soviet reality!

From letters, of which I receive fewer and fewer, barely

one or two a year, I have learned that most of my acquaintances who have suffered in the Gulag for the Truth have been arrested again. The good God knows that the condemnation weighing on the world today can be removed only by sacrifice, and he chooses those whom His Love designated before the ages. The suffering prisoners of conscience are the salt of the earth.

The Cause of Truth

The whole time, as much as circumstances allowed, I tried to contribute to the important and sacred work of assisting the wounded, persecuted Church of Lithuania, vilified in every way by the Soviets. That sacred task is being carried out by the *Chronicle of the Catholic Church in Lithuania*, reporting to everyone the injuries being inflicted on the Church, and urging all to remain faithful to Truth and Love. So I reproduced as much as I was able the *Chronicle of the Catholic Church in Lithuania* and other underground religious literature.

Twelve years ago, during my interrogation, I promised KGB Major Vytautas Pilelis that if God let me come back from the Gulag, I would again reproduce the *Chronicle*. With the help of God, I have been carrying out that promise. I rejoice and thank Almighty God that the issues of the *Chronicle* have become more and more substantial, and are approaching the 100 in number. A few years ago, a very noble individual extended to me the wish that I would be able to print issue 100. The wishes of holy people are fulfilled because their will coincides with the will of God, which consists in everyone's true happiness.

In the course of my work, I had occasion to meet people who were clearly in the spotlight of the KGB, under constant surveillance. There have been many exciting moments in those years, and throughout it all, my ignorance was made up for by our Good Father's hand. Everything always turned out well. Here are a few fragments from my life as a fugitive:

One time I visited some acquaintances whom I had visited more than once to drop off underground literature, and whom I knew were being particularly watched by the KGB. Listening devices had been installed in their apartment and telephone, their home was often being searched, the KGB was interrogating them and threatening to take care of them; their neighbors, KGB informers, kept an eye on everyone entering and leaving their apartment—in a word, the whole system of terror.

When I went to see them, I would hardly speak; everything I wanted to tell them I would write down so that the "ears" of the KGB would not hear. We used to converse *only* in writing. The KGB knows that *this is the only real way to remain unmonitored by the KGB.* Everyone should remember that! It is better to be careful so as not to help the KGB. It is obvious that one should immediately erase what one writes. If one wets that paper and rubs it, the writing fades, and if a drainpipe is available, you flush it.

Going to see those acquaintances, I would try to disguise myself, only I always left looking just as I had when I went in. But on this occasion, as I prepared to leave, I spontaneously put on a wig I had brought in with me, which used to change my appearance greatly, and donned a scarf, whereas I had come in wearing a beret. It was late evening and there was no one about. We took the elevator down. The corridor was in semi-darkness. After I had left the elevator, I still had to go down a flight of stairs to the exit. At the foot of the stairs, at the door, I saw standing two men who looked like criminals, one of them was sharpening a long knife on the steps while both of them observed me.

I could not run away. Without even pausing, I calmly went right toward them without paying any attention to them, as though I did not see them. I came to the door. Now they were behind me, off to one side. As luck would have it, the door would not open. In my heart was a calm that in moments like that, only the good God can grant. The thought occurred to me, "Let them stab me! I have completed my work, thank God!"

After a slight delay, I got the door open and without turning toward them, went out. Only after leaving did I realize that those men had probably been waiting for me to come out wearing a beret, as I had been wearing as I came into the apartment. The KGB often hires murderers to injure or kill those they are persecuting, but God's ways are not man's ways!

Another time, I was going to see some other acquaintances with underground literature. They were under KGB surveillance, but less than those mentioned above. When I arrived in the city where my friends lived, the thought suddenly occurred to me that I would need transportation to visit other people. Transportation was waiting for me, and when I arrived, I went someplace else instead. Later, I found out that precisely at that time, the militia had been looking for me at my original destination, they had questioned my friends, demanding to know what they knew about me. God helped me by inspiring me to go elsewhere. I am grateful to Him from the bottom of my heart.

More than once, with the help of God, I have been able to slip out from under the noses of the KGB. One time, as I was going to see some friends being persecuted by the KGB, their neighbors—KGB informers—saw me in the hallway, suspected me and immediately summoned the militia. They arrived in the yard by car, but I was able to disguise myself and evade them. On another occasion, the thought occurred to me to leave my apartment immediately. Barely had I gone out when the militia arrived to check the papers of the residents, something they had not done for decades.

Still another time, as I was going to some other people where I used to spend the night, I saw two militiamen standing on a side street. I often used to meet or see militiamen standing or lounging around, but this time, I clearly understood that they were waiting for me. Instead of going to the apartment, I stood aside unobtrusively and watched them. After a moment, it became obvious that they were waiting for me. They questioned the tenants about me, but by that time, I was far away. I thank everyone for their prayers. My poor brothers—the KGB and militia—how much trouble they have with me! Let us pray that in looking for me, they will find and come to love the Good Heavenly Father of us all.

Meanwhile, my brother's trial was approaching, and I went to Moscow to find my brother an attorney. Unfortunately, everyone here was also terrified of the KGB, I could not find an attorney. I remembered that in Moscow is the grave of a German Catholic ophthalmologist, Friedrich Josef Haas, who for fifty-one years served the most unfortunate, giving them the undivided love of his warm heart. Sergei Zheludkov, a Russian clergyman of fine memory, wrote to me in Siberia about him. I went to the former German cemetery to pray at the grave of F.J. Haas. In spite of the fact that he had gone to his eternal rest in 1853, there were flowers blooming on his grave. Love does not die! Passersby would frequently stop to pray at his grave. It was to this giant of love that I commended by brother's case:

"While living on earth, you gave yourself entirely to prisoners, patients and the exploited. Now in the glory of the Lord, you are able to do more. Be my brother's champion and defender!"

I knew that he would not abandon him. Oh how often in seeking help we forget those who are able and wish to help us most—those living in heaven. I was not disappointed. Sometime later, speaking by telephone with my brother's wife, I learned that the trial was to take place on May 24, 1987, that is the feast of the Blessed Virgin Mary, Help of Christians. F.J. Haas obtained for my brother the best Defender of all, the Blessed Mother! I rejoiced and was grateful!

I thanked Haas for his answer to my request, and went

through the park toward the Orthodox church where I was supposed to meet my friends. A man approached me along the path. As he drew near, he slowed down, stopped and with some surprise, looked at me from head to foot. I was going brunette, without any disguise. Hardly had I passed him when he turned and began to follow me.

I picked up my pace, and so did he. "Surely he hasn't recognized me? If only I could have time to warn my friends not to wait for me, and not to have any unpleasantness," I thought, hurrying toward the church. Thank God, the church was full of people with services in progress. I mingled with the crowd and donned a scarf and sweater which I had with me. I was also able to warn my friends. And I myself stood to one side near the side door where there were some low benches with some elderly ladies sitting on them.

The church was full of worshipers. After a while, I noticed two young men looking over everyone in the church with great interest. It was obvious that they were looking for someone. I commended myself to the will of God. "Fiat! I am ready!"

Before me was an icon of Our Lady of Vladimir. The thought occurred to me, "If they don't arrest me today, it means that the Blessed Mother wants me to write my recollections."

The two men slowly approached, and their eyes fixed intently on every face. In that moment, a little old lady sitting behind me stood up to leave, and I sat down in her place on a low bench next to some other old ladies. I lowered my head and pulled the scarf over my forehead; playing the role of a little old lady has saved me more than once. In any case, the young men probably did not even pay any attention to the little old ladies sitting next to the wall, because in an Orthodox church, only the very elderly and the sick sit. There are not many benches and the places are taken before the services.

I did not notice when the services ended and the people began to disperse. I helped the little old lady sitting next to me rise, and accompanying her, I left with a crowd of people by the side door. Once inside the churchyard, I went directly along the wall of the church, bent over, conversing with a little old lady. I brought her to and seated her in a bus.

We took a route different from the one by which I had come and I did not see my "tail", the detective. Upon reaching home, I immediately sat down to begin writing my recollections, and when I met my friends who had been in church at the time, they told me that it was the first time that they had seen the KGB scrutinizing people so blatantly, and they had feared greatly that I would be recognized.

Heroes of the Resistance:
Petras Paulaitis

Sometime later, the good God allowed me to meet Vladas Lapienis, at that time hiding from the KGB. In spite of his 79 years, Vladas was full of energy and Christian optimism. He worked hard without sparing himself. Vladas Lapienis, like our other prisoners of conscience, is suffering gladly for God and country, and that is a special sign of God's election. May the Almighty strengthen the prisoners of conscience on their difficult but honorable road of suffering in the Gulag!

I had the good fortune of seeing and having a good talk with our nation's heroic martyr, Petras Paulaitis,[1] who because of his love and loyalty to God and country, has spent thirty-five years in the Soviet Gulag. Just think, thirty-five years of inhuman suffering, degradation and dehumanization! But none of this enslaved his spirit; with good reason Scripture says, "The

---

[1]Petras Paulaitis (6/29/1904-2/19/1986), had been a member of the Lithuanian Underground operating against the Nazis. (At one point he was captured by the Gestapo, but escaped in a dramatic run for his life.) He continued his resistance activities when the Communists "liberated" Lithuania and, as Nijole puts it, "forgot" to leave. His sufferings in the Gulag over thirty-five years were so intense as to tempt him to suicide, which he resisted because of his faith in God.

truth shall make you free!"

Petras Paulaitis remained serene as a child, and his ac-commodation and love for everyone, even his enemies, moved one to tears. It was not without reason that even the chekists called him a standard of moral uprightness. Petras Paulaitis was a miracle of God's grace.

As his thirty-five years of suffering in the Gulag ended, one high-ranking chekist asked whether he didn't regret these thirty-five years stricken from his life. To this, Mr. Petras (so the prisoners called him) replied, "I am sorry only that being the son of a small nation, Lithuania, I did not know how to defend its freedom from the much more numerous Soviet occupation forces."

In the Gulag, prisoners of good will from every nation and shade of opinion deeply respected his moral greatness and hu-man warmth. He knew how to share his last bit of bread with prisoners who had been starved in punishment cells, how to lis-ten to, console and encourage each one of them. Prisoners of conscience of other nationalities envied us Lithuanians the fact that Petras was of our countrymen.

When prisoners transferred from one concentration camp to another met, the first question used to be, "How was Mr. Pe-tras?", and then they asked about their own countrymen. Young prisoners like the Ukrainian Zorvan Popadiuk, out of respect for Petras, learned Lithuanian in the concentration camp. From exile, Zorvan used to write letters to me in beautiful Lithuanian. That young man with his beautiful spirit, after nine years of suffering in the Gulag—in spite of the fact that while in prison he contracted tuberculosis and they removed part of his lungs while he was in exile—was given another fifteen years of incarceration by the "generous" hands of the KGB, just because he remained loyal to the truth.[2]

---

[2]Zorvan Popadiuk is presently confined in Ural Concentration Camp No. 36, together with the highly respected Father Alfonsas Svarinskas (618263, Permskaya obl., Chsovskoy *Rayon*, Kuchino, uchr.

After his thirty-five years in the Gulag, during the fall of 1982, Paulaitis was brought to the KGB dungeons in Vilnius. Here the KGB warned him not to try to write his memoirs, because he would disappear immediately without a trace.

"I know your little tricks, and how a year ago you killed Father Bronius Laurinavicius, tortured a whole list of priests and noble-hearted Lithuanians; you can shoot me on the spot."

The KGB began yelling at him to keep quiet; they would not let Petras finish speaking. Immediately they changed the subject and began asking where he wanted to live, whom he wanted to visit. Afraid to release him in the concentration camp uniform, they had him change into a suit at a nearby store. Here they outfitted him from head to toe using the money which Petras had earned while in the Gulag. Petras smiled, "The chekists suggested that I buy an imported suit, as though it were a better quality than the Soviet version."

After visiting a few relatives and friends, Petras settled in Kretinga. Each Sunday and Holy Day, he very devoutly assisted at the Sacrifice of the Mass, and received Holy Communion. Always and everywhere he was very modest and simple, and even though waves of pain now different from those in the Gulag kept pounding him, he knew how to preserve clarity and peace of soul. The KGB was able to poison the last days of his life, but they were never able to trample his human greatness and nobility.

His love and forgiveness even of those who falsely accused him, is best shown by the following incident. A young man who had for some time been with Petras in the Mordovia concentration camp came to visit Petras in Kretinga. Petras Paulaitis cared for him like a son, fed him, nurtured him, and watched over him. It was a joyful meeting, but after some time, a long,

VS-389-36). Serving sentence at the same location is third-termer Ukrainian prisoner of conscience Vasil Vasilevich Ovsenko. Zorvan's mother, unable to stand another enforced separation with her only son, died.

dirty, calumnious article about Petras' past, written in KGB style appeared, and under the article, the signature of his former protege in Mordovia.

How did Petras react to this? "If I met him, I would embrace him and beg, 'Don't take that road of lying, because it will kill you.' . . ." Petras was concerned only with the future of the unfortunate young man enslaved by the KGB.

When he wished to listen to Radio Free Europe or Vatican Radio broadcasts, and because of jamming on 2,672 cycles, he was unable to hear anything, with a bright peacefulness he would say, "We have only one thing left—we must try to be better!" Petras was accustomed to overcome any evil by good. Under torture and belittled, he knew how to forgive and to love.

The flame of Petras' life was extinguished February 19, 1986, like a flame on the altar, silently offering himself for others until death. He told me that he was praying that God would allow him to die like a bee, on the wing—working—so that he would not be a burden to anyone. God heard his prayer and called him to eternal joy where there would no longer be any death or moaning or pain. His large farmers' hands, which had done so much good for people, and with which even in the hell of the Gulag he had raised flowers, grew stiff on his breast in eternal rest. They clasped to his heart a rosary and a tri-color sash of independent Lithuania.

Only the poor KGB did not calm down. Their agents persecuted him even in death. They warned the priests not to inter him with religious services; they told the residents of Kretinga and the surrounding area not to attend the funeral; and they refused to allow students out of school on the day of the funeral. In spite of all the machinations of the powers of darkness, crowds of people accompanied the flower-decked casket of the deceased to the church in Kretinga. They gathered from every corner of Lithuania to pay their respects and to pray to this national hero and martyr.

Two months after the funeral, I visited the grave of Petras Paulaitis. It was a beautiful sunny day, the birds were singing, but a very strong wind was blowing. On Petras' grave grew a green sprig of rue, and varicolored blossoms, and among them stood a little basket of flowers from the handle of which a yellow, green and red ribbon was extended on to the grave. The tricolor of Independent Lithuania covered Petras' remains. It was surprising that the spiteful hand of the chekist had not torn it away.

I lighted some candles and recollected myself for prayer. In spite of the strong blasts of wind, the candles burned down to the end. Those lit on other graves immediately went out. It was difficult to take my leave.

Postscript

As I close these reminiscences, the struggle for truth in Lithuania continues. On December 9, 1986, raids took place in Vilnius, in a search of religious literature. They confiscated many books of a religious nature (bags of them), and typewriters. One man about forty years old, named Gediminas —I don't remember his surname—was arrested. He was accused of reproducing religious literature. Then, in early 1987, the authorities began to increase the jamming of foreign radio broadcasts—religious programs, Vatican Radio, even the broadcast of Mass....

In view of our continuing struggle, my account has been written very hastily, and I beg the reader to forgive me for my mistakes and handwriting. The style can be edited and abridged where necessary, but I would like to close with a spiritual reflection.

I often repeat the words of my confirmation patroness, Saint Theresa of the Child Jesus:

> I want nothing except what You want, O my Love,
> and as you want it,
> And let that which is mine because You give it
> be Thine because I return it,
> You gave me this, now take it back

that I may use it as pleases Thee.
Oh lead me as you will and know,
for You are truly Love!

The Sacrament of Confirmation was conferred on me,
June 10, 1945, by the Lithuanian martyr-bishop Vincentas Borisevicius. Thirty years later, to the day, they put me on trial. I
believe that the intercession of the martyr-bishop, Vincentas,
protected me and protects me still. How fortunate we are that
they saints and martyrs constantly pray for us, so that even the
weakest easily bear up under all trials.

I thank all those who have supported me and continue to
support me by their prayers. Let us pray for everyone, but especially those who lack love, who do not know God, for they
are our most unfortunate brothers and sisters.

Let us all be grateful and rejoice that Lithuania, during the
jubilee year (1983) of the redemption, was given two new martyrs, Father Alfonsas Svarinskas and Father Sigitas Tamkevicius.
These spiritual giants, powerful beacons of Christ's teaching for
many years, giving unstintingly of their strength, provided light
and warmth for thousands of Lithuanians, and now they will
light and warm millions throughout the world.

To suffer for Christ is a special sign of election. I would
like to end with this hymn of thanks:

You are God: We praise You;
You are the Lord: We acclaim you;
You are the eternal Father:
All creation worships You.
To you, all angels, all the powers of heaven,
Cherubim and Seraphim, sing in endless praise:
Holy, Holy, Holy
Lord God of power and might,
Heaven and earth are full of Your glory!